The Above Ground Railroad

THE ABOVE GROUND RAILROAD

The Story of the Matthew House
Movement in Canada

JOEY CLIFTON

TALL PINE PRESS

TALL PINE PRESS
94-11215 Jasper Avenue
Edmonton AB T5K 0L5
Canada

THE ABOVE GROUND RAILROAD
Written by Joey Clifton

All scripture quotations, unless otherwise indicated, are taken
from the Holy Bible, Today's New International Version®, TNIV®.
Copyright© 2001, 2005 by International Bible Society.® Used by
permission of Zondervan. All rights reserved worldwide.
www.zondervan.com

Printed in the United States.
Photography: By Joey Clifton, except photo on Page 90 by Christine Walsh.
Design: Dianne Eastman.
Text has been set in Berling.

Library and Archives Canada Cataloguing in Publication

Clifton, Joey
       The above ground railroad : the story of the Matthew
House Movement in Canada / Joey Clifton.

ISBN 978-0-9810149-1-3

       1. Matthew House--History. 2. Refugees--Services for--
Canada. I. Title.

BV4466.C55 2012   261.8'3280971   C2012-903057-0

DEDICATION AND ACKNOWLEDGEMENTS

This book is dedicated to the people who welcome Jesus as they welcome refugees into their homes—the Matthew House staff and volunteers in Ontario and Quebec. We want to draw attention to the thousands who flee persecution along global highways that are similar to those who traveled underground between the U.S and Canada. Why use the expression Above Ground? It's because this Movement is not secret. We know in real time what tragedies fill our world. People from broken and war-torn nations arrive in our cities within weeks and months after we hear on the news about their disasters.

The story of the Matthew House Movement is about refugees being welcomed, not just symbolically. Those who come to live at one of the five Matthew Houses scattered around Ontario and Quebec are invited into, no…they are adopted into families of churches and individuals who follow Jesus. Some of these champions of peace and community are named in this book. There are many others who have been, and continue to be, the presence of Christ to refugees, although their names are not recorded here. The book is dedicated to their humble service also.

We want to acknowledge Anne Woolger, who leads the parade of missioners who faithfully welcome strangers into their lives. It was Anne who first said 'Yes Lord—send me' to establish the first Matthew House in Toronto. Anne loves the Lord. She loves refugee claimants. She loves the church. We are happy to call her our friend. Anyone who knows her, knows she doesn't take 'no' for an answer. Anne gets things done; amazing things get done when she is involved.

We want to acknowledge those who knelt, prayed, gave their time and resources from the beginning to make visible the words of Matthew 25:35-36 by providing bricks and mortar, bread and water, hugs and tears, laughter and authentic Christian community that also are foundational to the Matthew House Movement. Thousands of refugees continue to be welcomed into hope, joy and freedom because of your hard work. Thank you, Anne. Thank you Matthew House staff, volunteers, donors and advocates.

Joey, thank you for giving so much of your time to help tell this mission narrative so that others might follow the examples set forth in it. Thank you for sharing your special gift of storytelling in word and photograph. Tom Ogburn and Brian McAtee, faithful friends and missioners who were willing to invest in the Kingdom without promise of success—who only ask for the opportunity to love through action. Thank you.

First Baptist Church Oklahoma City, your generosity and commitment to missions funded Joey's trip to Canada and you lifted prayer on his behalf. Thank you. First Baptist Church, Huntsville, Alabama. You believed in this project and committed the first dollars to make it happen. The Cooperative Baptist Fellowship, made up of "free and faithful" friends back home, you were always ready to roll up your sleeves and help, or get on your knees and pray. We want to acknowledge special friends like Linda, Judy, Beth, Elizabeth, Amanda, Bill, Ruby, Gwen, Carla, Kathy, Joe, Scott, Eleanor, Stu, Larry, Linda, Joyce and Nathan. We want to thank our team and coaches for putting up with our stuff and for loving us anyway.

Laurie Barber, the Gentleman Apostle among us, able to inspire men and women to follow their dreams and visions as the Spirit leads them, you were instrumental in the Matthew House Movement in Canada. Thank you for the time you gave as you quietly guided us through the editing process and for inspiring the book's title. Clarence and Nancy Webb, you gave graciously and lovingly of yourselves by helping refugee claimants and those who serve them. We thank the many Canadian Christian churches and individuals who continue to support, pray for and partner with the Matthew Houses of Ontario and Quebec. Thank you Ken and Joyce Bellous for publishing the story through Tall Pine Press.

Tim and Julie McCoy, lifelong friends, closer than family, true apprentices of our Lord Jesus: Words cannot express our gratitude for your support and participation in this movement.

We want to especially thank our children, Rebecca Joy and Jon Marc, who have at times wondered what land they were from and whether they actually lived at Matthew House. We love you.

Merci,
Marc and Kim Wyatt
CBF Field Personnel
http://www.cbfinternationals.org/
Project Producers

CONTENTS

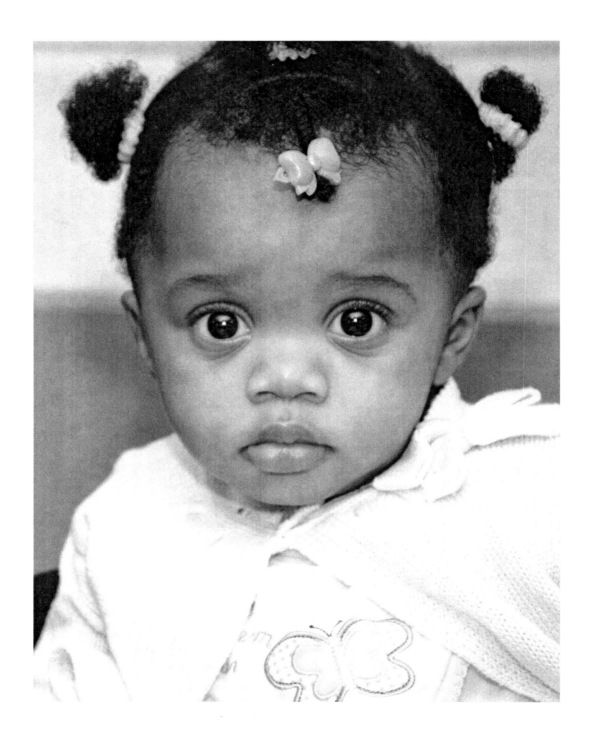

PREFACE

The Matthew House Story inspires, challenges and motivates us to create change through the power of God's Holy Spirit. It's a story about welcoming newcomers. The following pages describe one woman's call to ministry and the exponential increase of stories from families whose lives have been beautifully altered through the perfected art and ministry of welcoming, which is based on Jesus' call in Matthew 25:34-36,

"Then the King will say to those on his right, 'Come, you who are blessed by my Father; take your inheritance, the kingdom prepared for you since the creation of the world. For I was hungry and you gave me something to eat, I was thirsty and you gave me something to drink, I was a stranger and you invited me in. I needed clothes and you clothed me, I was sick and you looked after me, I was in prison and you came to visit me."

My own encounter with her call to ministry came as I led a group of students from the United States to Matthew House Toronto in 2003. During that trip, I began to understand the powerful impact of Anne Woolger and the Matthew House family.

Unknown to me at the time, one day I would be a newcomer to Canada. When I arrived, I was not welcomed officially by Matthew House staff, yet I felt the influence of Canadian Christians, specifically in the Matthew House Movement, as I settled here with my family. In 2003, I didn't know about the partnership between Matthew House and the Canadian Baptists of Ontario and Quebec (CBOQ.) I was looking for adventure in a new land. Following God's call, my family and I moved from North Carolina to Toronto. In 2006, I began working for CBOQ and partnering with the great work of the Matthew House Movement.

Since arriving in this country, I've learned that Canadian Christians have been welcoming newcomers for hundreds of years. During the American Civil War, the Underground Railroad brought slave families to southern Ontario—to a free country. Chinese refugees also found their way to Canada over the last 150 years. After every outbreak of war and following natural disasters all around the world, many more refugees make their way to Canada. Welcoming newcomers is Gods' work. For Canadians, it is work carried out, in part, through the Matthew House Movement.

This book is a story of one woman, Anne Woolger, and hundreds of people who journey with her to spread the Matthew House Movement. They inspire us to consider the Christ-given challenge to feed the hungry and invite in the strangers that stand at our door. Joey

Clifton captures the essence of the Movement and has highlighted the intentional ministry of individuals and organizations who work together to sow the seeds of this new ministry. Thank you, Joey. I wish to express deep gratitude to Anne Woolger, Marc & Kim Wyatt, the Cooperative Baptists and hundreds more Canadians, from other denominations, for leading the way in living the message of Christ. Let us hear the call to embrace the people that God is bringing to North America.

Tim McCoy
Executive Minister
Canadian Baptists of Ontario & Quebec

CHAPTER 1

THE REFUGEE HIGHWAY

Anne Woolger

I sat across the room from Anne Woolger in her modest, tidy Toronto home. A small tape recorder sat between us on the coffee table. She sat on the couch, her glasses propped on top of her head as she told me her story. At times, she folded one leg beneath her; at other times, she was too animated to sit still. In our two hour conversation, she laughed a lot. She cried too—some of her stories are filled with tragedy and sorrow; sometimes she wept at the overwhelming wonder of the way God works. Occasionally she spoke fast; sometimes slowly, as if she was right in the room with the people whose stories she shared with me. Once in a while, her rhythm increased, as if she couldn't get the story and its message out quickly enough.

Several times during the morning she moved away from the main narrative and said, "Let me tell you one little God-story." From there she launched into remarkable, specific ways that God answered prayer or worked out a circumstance that only God could manage. Finally, I interrupted her. "Anne, this story you're sharing with me is not a series of little God-stories. It is one big God Story. There is no doubt in my mind that God's hand has been part of every moment."

I'm about to get ahead of myself. Anne's enthusiasm does that. You'll read more of her story in the next chapter. For now, let me share one of her many God-stories; it's the one that helped set the course of her life.

A CHANCE ENCOUNTER

During a quiet time one morning while she was attending Queen's University in Kingston Ontario, Anne found herself reading Proverbs 31. In verses 8 and 9, the king says to his son, "Speak up for those who cannot speak for themselves, for the rights of all who are destitute. Speak up and judge fairly; defend the rights of the poor and needy." It is a moment she still vividly remembers. "The words jumped out at me," she said. "It was as if God said to me, 'This is your calling'."

A moment of calling is a holy moment, one's bright light or burning bush. But often the details are far from clear. In Anne's case, she was wondering if she should study journalism. Was she to fulfill her new calling through the written word? She also thought about becoming a missionary. Was this the way God wanted her to "Speak up for those who cannot speak up for themselves?"

To test out the possibility of missions, after university Anne spent a year in Japan teaching

English. She remembers thinking, "I could do this." Could and should, however, are two different things. Was this what God wanted for her life? When she came back from Japan, she entered Toronto's Tyndale Seminary to pursue a Masters of Theological Studies degree. While there, she took a field placement doing outreach to international students at nearby York University. One of the members of her group was a young, blind, native Canadian woman from the far north who volunteered her time to make other people feel welcome. Anne said, "I was so impressed with this girl. She had so many things against her, yet she wanted to reach out to others." Anne decided to invite her to dinner, to get to know her better. When she called, the young friend quickly agreed but told Anne that she had two friends visiting her from her home in northern Canada. So it became a dinner for four rather than for two.

One of the guests was an eighteen-year-old Asian refugee. Because he found Anne's home to be an inviting and safe place, he shared his story after dinner. His family escaped great persecution on a boat with other people from Asia. North Americans refer to them as "boat people." On the long, difficult journey, his brother and sister died of starvation. Another brother was shot and blinded. As Anne listened to this young man's story, she told me that her heart was aching. "I wanted him to hurry up and tell the happy ending about arriving in Canada, being welcomed…living happy ever after."

Instead, the young refugee described his first few days, weeks and months in Canada as the most difficult, most painful part of the journey. Anne thought, "After all he has been through, could this really be the most painful part?" When he arrived in Canada, an immigration officer took his family to an old motel unit close to the airport, gave them a little money and said he would return the next week. They didn't speak the language. They didn't know how to work the stove. They didn't know where to shop or how to communicate their needs. Eventually, they were taken to northern Ontario. At his new school he was different from the other kids and eventually, he was ostracized. He told us: "I used to cry myself to sleep at night, wishing I was back home in the killing fields."

This eye-opening encounter with a refugee set a new course for Anne's life. Of course, it wasn't just a chance encounter. If we believe God is ultimately at work in the lives of those who seek him, of those he calls, we believe that life changing events, which further his kingdom, are full of purpose. Without realizing it at the time, God was filling in the details of her call. His call and direction are not always a blinding light such as Paul experienced, or a burning bush where Moses removed his sandals. More often, they are gentle urgings of the Holy

Spirit as we study scripture or converse with others. It is up to us to hear and respond.

Anne remembers thinking that night, "Something is wrong here. While I'm in Seminary, at least I can do something to help refugees feel welcome." And she did.

REFUGEES AMONG US

My wife and I sat with Stan and Heather Mantle on the hard, wooden front pew of the Sandwich First Baptist Church in Sandwich, Ontario. Pacing across the platform before us, Dr. Colin Smith, pastor of the church, gave us a private history lesson about slave abuse in the United States South and the resulting Underground Railroad that led them to Canada. Sandwich First Baptist is the oldest black congregation in Canada. It was formed by escaped slaves who fled their brutal masters and made the treacherous trek north. Here they found freedom and a place of welcome.

During our tour, Pastor Smith showed us the escape hatches on either side of the sanctuary. Newly escaped slaves would stand close to these covered openings in the floor, just in case a bounty hunter came looking for them. If a bounty hunter showed up, they would slide down the small hole and crawl beneath the church, to escape through a tunnel that led down to the Detroit River. Beneath the rug on the platform was another escape exit that, when lifted, revealed a set of steps that descended to the tunnel. Despite their new found freedom, many continued to live in fear, afraid the threats they left behind would catch up with them.

The Underground Railroad was maintained by a loose system of religious and ethnic groups that moved the black refugees north toward freedom. The underground, or secret nature of this pipeline kept refugees safe along their journey. Although historians can't say with certainty how many black refugees made their way to Canada, many believe the number approaches 40,000.

Today, over 42 million people have been forcefully displaced from their homes due to war and famine. Others flee their home countries because of serious human rights abuses. These refugees currently number 16 million. The movement of refugees across the globe in search of a new safe home is called the Refugee Highway. Laurie Barber, Director of Missional Initiatives for the Canadian Baptists of Ontario and Quebec, uses the term the Above Ground Railroad for this stream of displaced people. A pipeline of refugees from all over the world continues to enter Canada, despite efforts by some to shut down the flow. Today, this railroad is no longer secret. Refugees continue above ground to find their way to a new land to escape abuse, suffering and injustice. As in the days of the Southern slaves, they search for a place where they are welcomed and accepted.

We also have to remember that during World War II many countries, including Canada, failed to offer asylum to Jewish refugees, which greatly contributed to the death toll of the Holocaust. In order to make sure these mistakes are not repeated, the 1951 Geneva Convention (sometimes called the Refugee Convention) was developed. According to this Convention, a refugee is:

A person who is outside his or her home country and who has a well-founded fear of being persecuted for reasons of race, religion, nationality, membership of a particular social group or political opinion.

In 1993, Canada became the first country to recognize that women can be persecuted for their gender as well. Due to Canada's historic commitment to assuring the mistakes of the past are not revisited, it has become an important end point for the Refugee Highway, a final destination for those who have been persecuted and displaced.

There are two types of refugees that make their way to Canada each year: Sponsored Refugees and Claimant Refugees. A Sponsored Refugee is one who has found his or her way to a visa post or United Nations High Commission for Refugees (UNHCR) office where they wait in camps or low-income housing for approval and resettlement. When they are resettled they are provided government or group sponsorship (such as a church) to help them make the transition as smoothly as possible. Claimant Refugees, on the other hand, find their way to another country on their own and ask for asylum. Many of these people have no way to access a visa post or UNHCR office or perhaps don't know such an office exists. Rather than turning these asylum seekers aside and forcing them to return to the dangers of their own country, Canada receives many of them until it can determine the legitimacy of their claim. Although these refugees are eligible for some financial support, there are no government-run agencies or sponsors to assist them on arrival and they are simply numbered among the homeless. Their survival is left up to them.

Enough about definitions. Thousands of refugees live throughout Canada. Some were sponsored. Others show up at Canada's borders looking for a safe place to live and a welcoming hand. They've left everything behind. No one speaks their language. They discover that their education, and many are highly educated, does not guarantee them a job in the new country. Refugees typically are not valued or wanted. They live in fear and confusion. Said Bangura, a Matthew House staff member, came to Canada from Sierra Leone where over 12,000 civilians including women and children had their arms and legs amputated as a result of the bloody civil war which left several thousand dead. The Refugee Highway, he says, is "a very traumatic, fearful, bitter and painful experience most of the time."

Anne Woolger shared one such incident with me. She received a call from a police officer at Toronto Airport in the middle of the night. He had found a very pregnant woman with a four-year-old child wandering through the airport. She couldn't speak English and was crying. Eventually, the police officer was able to look at her papers and discovered that she had arrived from Sudan seeking asylum. She had been wandering in the airport for eight hours, no idea where to go or what to do.

Stories I heard from others are just as telling. In one incident Jim McNair, a refugee worker in Ft. Erie, Ontario was transporting a young refugee in his truck. As they went through a school zone, the young man ducked down beneath the dash with a great deal of fear.

"What's wrong?" Jim asked.

"Didn't you see that policeman getting ready to shoot us?" he replied.

Indeed, there was a policeman there with a gun pointed directly at Jim's truck. It was a radar gun. This young man came from a place where policemen, soldiers and other people with guns often shot and brutalized innocent people.

On another occasion Jim was giving a young refugee woman driving lessons. As they started down a long wooded lane, she said, "We shouldn't go down there should we?"

Jim said, "I don't understand. Why not?"

"There might be men with guns hiding in the woods," she replied.

She came from a country where women and children were often kidnapped or killed on such isolated stretches of road.

Knowledge of refugees in Canada may mean little to us until we put faces and stories to the term refugee. Kim Wyatt, another refugee worker you'll meet later in the book, said: "When the term refugee or newcomer becomes Hiwot, Jacob, or Angeline it becomes a very different thing. It becomes personal." When Anne Woolger met her first refugee, she came to know what refugee meant not by memorizing a definition, but by empathizing with his story. It is not until we choose to open our arms to those who come to us for help and asylum that we understand the need and plight of refugees in North America.

GOD HAS A HEART FOR REFUGEES

Anne Woolger discovered God's heart for refugees in Proverbs 31, although at the time she didn't connect "those who cannot speak for themselves" or "the poor and needy" with refugees. She soon discovered that when refugees come to a new country they often can't speak the language or understand the red-tape of the immigration system. They have no place to stay and little means to find proper shelter. They need someone to speak for them. In addition, when they flee their home country, they often have to leave everything. They come to their new land destitute and lonely. They need the help of God's people.

In the Old Testament we read that during a great famine in the days of Jacob, he and his whole family moved to Egypt. They were displaced people. Some years later, the Egyptians enslaved and brutalized the Hebrew people. Under Moses' leadership, the refugees fled the land and the Egyptian army gave chase. Refugees today are no different. They flee a difficult or life-threatening situation in search of a new home.

God cares about the displaced person. One of the new laws for the Hebrew people, as God formed them as a nation, spelled out how they should respond to the alien among them: "When foreigners reside among you in your land, do not mistreat them. The foreigners residing among you must be treated as your native-born. Love them as yourself, for you were foreigners in Egypt." (Leviticus 19:33-34) Once settled, these new citizens of the Promised Land set up cities of refuge so individuals might "flee there and find protection from the avenger of blood." (Joshua 20:3)

If you were to search for the word refugee in the Bible you wouldn't find it. But if you searched for the related word refuge, multiple occurrences are found. For example, when King Saul sought to kill David, he fled to the land of the Philistines. Later, after his refugee ordeal was over, he composed a song.

> The LORD is my rock, my fortress and my deliverer;
> My God is my rock, in whom I take refuge,
> My shield and the horn of my salvation.
> He is my stronghold, my refuge and my saviour--
> From violent people you save me.
> (2 Samuel 22:2-3)

Repeatedly, David returns to this theme in the Psalms because he understood the fear, shame, loneliness and anger that refugees feel. He wanted justice and retribution on his enemies. He, like all refugees, wanted freedom from the never-ending fear. Millions of refugees around the world today join David in his prayer.

> LORD my God, I take refuge in you;
> save and deliver me from all who pursue me,
> or they will tear me apart like a lion
> and rip me to pieces with no one to rescue me.
> (Psalm 7:1-2)

Who will step forward to rescue the refugee, those needing a safe haven, if not the people of God? In recent years, many governments, including Canada, have narrowed the doors of entrance in order to limit the flow of those seeking refuge. They fear terrorism or the drain on their economy. They choose to restrict the law instead of opening the arms of grace. Does turning away those in desperate need express the heart of God? Perhaps there are some risks to opening our arms to refugees, but God calls us to take the action of compassion in faith. He asks us to trust him.

We forget sometimes that Jesus and his family were refugees. After his birth, Herod sought to kill Jesus. His family fled to Egypt. The Son of God, God incarnate, fled his home looking for a place of safety. I sometimes wonder what his years in Egypt were like. Did he live in a refugee camp? Did someone take Joseph, Mary and Jesus into their home? Did anyone care that they were strangers in a foreign land?

Eventually, all of us will one day stand before Jesus when he sits on his throne (Matthew 25:31-46) and divides us into two groups: the sheep and the goats. The sheep are those who fed the hungry, gave drink to the thirsty, housed the stranger, clothed the naked, cared for the sick and visited the prisoner. Jesus said, "Truly I tell you, whatever you did for one of the least of these brothers and sisters of mine, you did for me." To the sheep Jesus promises blessing and eternal life.

The goats are those who failed to care for the hungry, thirsty, homeless, naked, sick and incarcerated. They are the ones who turned their back on those seeking refuge. Jesus said, "whatever you did not do for one of the least of these, you did not do for me." The consequence of such uncaring attitudes is severe.

These are harsh and difficult words. Every refugee—the poor, hungry and homeless person seeking asylum and a place to call home—represents Jesus fleeing to safety in Egypt. The question is: "Are we there to welcome him?" If we choose to shut our doors or turn away, we do so to Jesus.

The Matthew House Response

After Anne Woolger began working with refugees in Toronto (read the whole story in the next chapter), she began to notice that they were coming from all the people groups she had studied about in her Seminary classes. A light went on in her head. She could fulfill her call to missions right there in Toronto. "I wondered," she said, "Who is reaching out to welcome all these people?" The answer was, "No one." I realized the world was arriving on our doorstep, often in desperate need and I asked myself: "Where are God's people?" She began to dream about a shelter she would eventually call "Matthew House" that would welcome refugees in Jesus' name.

The Matthew House Movement, as you will see in the following chapters is God's people at work. Matthew 25, the call of Jesus "to minister unto the least of these" is at the heart of the movement. The Movement is Christians responding to the needs of refugees by providing them housing, support and encouragement. It is Christian people welcoming displaced and persecuted people in the name of Jesus.

Although the movement is based on our call in Matthew 25:31-46, a closer look reveals that the entire chapter is about the Kingdom of God. Jesus begins with the words, "The kingdom of heaven will be like. . . ." First, it will be like virgins waiting for the bridegroom with their oil lamps. Those prepared with extra oil are let into the wedding. We are called to be ready to serve the bridegroom. (25:4) Second, the kingdom of heaven is like a man who goes on a journey and entrusts his property to servants. Those that faithfully invest and use what the master gives them are blessed and share "in the Master's happiness." (25:21) Finally, during the separation of the sheep and goats, those who respond to the call to minister are granted the inheritance of God's kingdom. (25:34) The Matthew House movement is the kingdom of God—the preparation, faithful service, and compassion of God's people. The kingdom of God,

> Is it not to share your food with the hungry
> and to provide the poor wanderer with shelter—
> when you see the naked, to clothe them,
> and not to turn away from your own flesh and blood?

Then your light will break forth like the dawn,
and your healing will quickly appear;
then your righteousness will go before you,
and the glory of the LORD will be your rear guard.
Then you will call, and the LORD will answer;
you will cry for help, and he will say: Here am I.

If you do away with the yoke of oppression,
with the pointing finger and malicious talk,
and if you spend yourselves in behalf of the hungry
and satisfy the needs of the oppressed,
then your light will rise in the darkness,
and your night will become like the noonday."
(Isaiah 58:7-10)

From Persecution to a Place of Hope

Jalal* was a successful doctor in his home country. One night secret police arrived at his door. He was imprisoned and tortured. After his release, threats continued. Terrified, he knew he had to escape fast. A long wait at an embassy could cost his life. An "agent" offered swift passage to a safe country for a fee. Desperate, he paid it and soon found himself on a plane en route to Toronto.

After asking for asylum at the airport he was sent out with no guidance as to what to do next. Alone and penniless, he did not know where to turn for help. His first night was spent on the street. Eventually he found a city homeless shelter where he slept on a floor mat among dozens of men with addictions and other problems. His few possessions were stolen. Already traumatized, this experience furthered Jalal's state of despair.

A few days later a concerned homeless shelter worker directed him to Matthew House. Here he was warmly welcomed and helped by caring staff and volunteers. Gradually his dignity was restored and his journey back to wholeness and hope began. Today, Dr. Jalal is successfully established and working in the medical field.

*Not his real name
Taken from **A place of hope at the end of the refugee highway**,
a brochure for Matthew House, Toronto.

32

CHAPTER **2**

MATTHEW HOUSE TORONTO

Anne Woolger knew that refugees coming to Canada needed to be welcomed. As a result, she decided, "While I'm here in Seminary, at least I can do something to help refugees feel welcome." How many times do we say that we're going to do something about this or that and never do? How many times do we feel the tug of God at our lives and know we must get involved to make a difference, but let it slide until the Spirit's urging diminishes within us? As we learned in the last chapter, God calls his children to action, to care for the vulnerable and displaced of our world. It's easy for us to respond in the affirmative, "Yes, Lord. I hear your call." It's much more difficult and rare for us to respond to that call with a fervent passion that not only begins, but also follows through by taking action.

Anne chose the way of action without delay. The day after spending an evening meal with her new refugee friend she looked up the word refugee in the phone book, found an organization called the Refugee Information Center and called to volunteer. Most of us, myself included, might see a need. We might hear the urge of God's call, but rather than respond, we sit back and tell ourselves: "What can I do? I don't even know where to begin. I can't do anything about that because I don't know much about refugees or where to even find them." We are awakened from slumber by Anne's response that it's really quite simple. If we seek to make a difference and are truly willing to act, God will direct.

GOD'S DIRECTION

Just before Easter, during the first year she started to volunteer there, the director of Refugee Information Center asked Anne if she knew of a place where refugees could go for Easter services that would be welcoming to them. A church that welcomes refugees? Is there such a place? Anne began her search and found Danforth Baptist Church that already had a refugee support group. She found like-minded people at Danforth and began attending there.

After graduating from seminary, the church asked Anne to be part of a team set aside to start a new church in an economically troubled area of Toronto. When she agreed, the church sent a group of three people to England for the summer to take a church planting course.

The church planting model they studied proposed that the three-member team move into the area where they wanted to start the church, become part of the community and be a light for Christ before even beginning a new work. This required that Anne find a job. Although she was willing to do anything, she didn't have any idea where to start. Her friend,

Nadine, who was part of the team from Canada, prayed specifically for Anne, "God, I pray that you lead Anne to the job that's just perfect for her." She then told Anne that she felt that her prayer was prophetic.

When Anne returned from England, she and the team settled in South Riverdale where they wanted to start the church. She prayed continuously for God's direction. On the first morning after moving to her new home she remembers praying, "Lord show me where to work." Then she set out walking down the street. She soon came to a building called the Neighbourhood House attached to a church building. She had no idea what it was but she walked in to find out.

Adults and children moved up and down the stairs in a beehive of activity. Anne found someone that appeared to work there and told her she was looking for a job. She was directed to a woman named Sheri who brought Anne into her office. A little child wandered into her office as well. Sheri placed him on her knee and said to Anne,

"Do you like children?"

"Well, yes," Anne replied.

"Would you like a job in our daycare?" Sheri asked.

"Oh, really?" Anne said, stunned and confused.

"Do you want it? Do you want it?" Sheri persisted.

Anne had no idea where she was or what was happening in this place and needed to slow down this conversation a bit.

"What is this place?" she asked.

"Oh, we're a shelter for homeless people. We have three floors. One is for abused women and children, one for homeless Canadians, and one is for refugees."

When Anne heard the word refugees her ears perked up. "I would love a job on the refugee floor if there is an opening," she said.

"If you take a job in the daycare there might be an opening in a few months," Sheri said.

Although Anne didn't take the job immediately (she was too stunned for that), she prayed about it for a day and accepted the job in the shelter's daycare the next day. Within three months, January 1989, a job opened on the refugee floor. Anne was given the position. The community shelter proved to be the perfect training ground for Anne's future work. Canada was bringing in about 13,000 government sponsored refugees a year and they wanted the shelter personnel to be trained. Anne joined the community shelter staff in training events on how to deal with refugees in trauma and how to help settle them.

At the shelter, Anne worked with government sponsored refugees and refugee claimants. When the government sponsored refugees arrived, they were immediately given refugee status, set up with housing, given basic new furniture and vouchers for clothing, and provided with Canadian families to host them. They arrived knowing they were safe and could stay in the country.

Occasionally, an empty bed on her floor was filled with a non-sponsored refugee claimant. These people were classified as part of the city's homeless population. They were often from the same countries as sponsored refugees and had the same horrific stories. But they were unlucky because they weren't able to access a visa post and had to be smuggled to Canada. Anne began to call this group the "hitchhikers." They arrived, terrified they would not be allowed to stay. They were given basic welfare and basic health coverage, but they weren't given housing, furniture or clothing vouchers, and they were unsure if they would ultimately be granted refugee status. In essence, they were left to their own devices and often ended up on the streets with no place to turn for help.

God placed Anne in this homeless shelter where she could see first-hand the needs of refugee claimants. She referred to that time and said, "That's when this passion started to really arise. I was seeing the most hurting people of our world." The Iraq-Iran war was going on at the time . She was seeing people from these countries as well as Afghanistan and Somalia. She knew a welcoming place was needed where these refugee claimants could experience the love of God; a Christian shelter where she could live out her calling to "speak up for those who cannot speak for themselves, for the rights of the destitute." God called Anne; then he gave her a passion.

Do you see how, once we take a step of faith and act on God's urging in our lives, God takes over and leads us on a wonderful journey we could not have imagined. In Anne's case, she chose to respond to God's urging by volunteering. The director of her volunteer placement sent her to find a church. The church embraced and trained her to help start another church. God then placed her in the right location and answered her prayer by providing the perfect job where she could learn all about refugees and nurse the growing passion within her. The journey we take with God is always exciting, but it must start with a step of faith, a response and a deep trust that God will guide along the way.

A Growing Understanding

During Anne's seven years at the community shelter, she took one summer in Strasbourg, France to attend a course in international human rights law. She also became the community shelter's refugee representative on the Toronto Refugee Affairs Council and the Canadian Council of Refugees. She discovered that there were few churches involved with helping refugees. When she approached Canadian Baptists about this omission, they invited her to be their representative on the Inter-Church Committee for Refugees under the umbrella of the Canadian Council of Churches. Twice in those years she represented the Inter-Church Committee for Refugees at the United Nations High Commission for Refugees (UNHCR) in Geneva. In these settings Anne learned a great deal about the difficulties and struggles of refugees on the Refugee Highway. She learned about international systems and political barriers that hinder people from receiving aid.

Yet no one truly understands what it's like to be a refugee unless they experience it firsthand. She took vacations abroad to refugee producing countries, which included a trip to the Kurdish enclave in Northern Iraq where she visited families of refugees she had befriended in Toronto. Before leaving on this trip she prayed, "Lord, help me learn more of what it feels like to be a refugee." She had a wonderful time in Iraq. She was warmly welcomed by the Kurds, but during their return through Turkey, policemen knocked on her door in the middle of the night, waking her and her roommate. The women were interrogated because their passports showed they had been in Iraq. The next day her roommate asked, "Anne, why did you pray that prayer?!" While there, she took the time to visit the UNHCR office in Ankara, Turkey and saw how difficult it is for refugees to access help overseas.

Training, education and knowledge are all important in working with refugees, but not all of us will have, or even need to have, the training and experiences God provided for Anne. What is needed for all of us is a heart that wants to understand, a deep desire to empathize with fears, frustrations and losses that refugees experience. We can begin our own education by praying Anne's prayer, "Lord, help me learn what it feels like to be a refugee."

Baptist Partners

As Anne began to share her vision for a refugee house that would welcome claimants in Jesus' name, people began to come along side her. One of the first groups was the Canadian

Baptists of Ontario and Quebec (CBOQ). When she asked them, "What are the Baptists doing for refugees?" their response was, "Do you have any suggestions?" "Yeah," she said, "We could open up a shelter for them and welcome them in Jesus' name." The CBOQ leadership had no hesitation. "Tell us what you need," they said; a partnership was born.

Several people formed a working group that later became the Matthew House Board. This group set out without any model to use. Their first thought was to find a house, but it was extremely difficult to raise money for something that didn't yet exist. One day, Anne attended a meeting at the CBOQ offices in downtown Toronto. At the time, their offices were housed in an old, beautiful, former Anglican Church building. As she walked down one of the halls she discovered to her amazement that it was lined with furnished bedrooms. "I was seeing refugees filling those beds," she said.

Anne found out that the 14 beds were used to house visitors that come to Toronto for meetings. The rooms were often full during the winter months but remained empty during the summer. Someone suggested to Anne that she develop a proposal to use the beds for refugees during the summer, sort of a pilot project. This was a rather radical idea, but Anne presented the proposal anyway.

Eventually, the proposal was discussed at an annual assembly meeting. "No one knew me," she said. "I sat in the background and let others do all the talking." Like all good Baptists, this group needed to work through the details, questions and the fear of something so radically new. For some, the initial reaction was, "What?! Refugees in our space?!" Others wanted answers to tough questions so they could make an informed decision. Anne remembers one intimidating man who asked several difficult questions. Eventually, the assembly agreed that Anne should meet with the people who actually worked in the building. If those who worked in the building were okay with the idea, perhaps they could work something out. Anne left the assembly meeting somewhat encouraged.

The next meeting took place in the building itself. Employees sat with Anne in the large dining room around one of the tables. "I was scared," she said. They asked more questions about her idea and vision. They asked hypothetical questions, for which she had few good answers. The man from the assembly that had asked so many pertinent, difficult questions was also there that day. This time Anne was intimidated, not by his questions, but by his silence. He said nothing. Finally, the employees agreed to consider the idea, but they would need a liaison, someone to work with Anne and monitor the situation. At that point, Anne's intimidator raised his hand. "I'll do it," he said. Anne was petrified, "Oh, no!"

As it turned out, that man was Larry Matthews, Editor of the Canadian Baptist magazine. When everyone left the meeting except him and Anne, he came and sat next to her. "I just want you to know," he said, "I'm 110% behind this idea. I'll do everything I can to help you get refugees in this building." Although Anne didn't know Larry personally at this point, he became one of her biggest supporters. Because he was Editor, he had access to computer equipment that could be used to produce church bulletin inserts, which they used to recruit volunteers. Eventually, Larry became the founding chair of the Board.

Anne's vision for refugees became a reality in the form of "pilot projects" that were carried out during the summers of 1992 and 1993. For two summers they housed about 50 refugees who lived and dined among the Baptist leaders. The first summer, Anne was able to get a leave from her job at the community shelter. One of her first volunteers, Christine Martin, initially offered to volunteer two days a week. By the end of the second week, when refugees began arriving, Anne was overwhelmed; Christine agreed to come five days a week. The next summer, Christine worked full-time so Anne didn't have to take a summer leave from her regular job. But because Anne was working shifts at the community shelter, she was still able to commit large chunks of time to the project.

Anne shared the powerful impact Canadian Baptists had on the success of Matthew House because of the support of people like John Wilton (then head of the CBOQ) and Larry Matthews. "It got Matthew House known right from the start which may not have happened if we had been in some corner of the Province in a little house." Did everything always go smoothly? No. But the people of God partnered together to meet the needs of refugee claimants because it was the right thing to do. Responding to God's direction in our lives means treading in places that intimidate us; things don't always go smoothly. It is during such times that we see the ability of God to manoeuvre us through the fears and uncertainties of the challenge he's called us to carry out.

The Vision Tarries and Dark Days

After the summer of 1993, CBOQ sold their downtown building and moved to their new location in east Toronto. As a result, the Matthew House project was put on hold while the Board looked for a new home. The community shelter offered Anne a promotion but she turned it down because she firmly believed the permanent Matthew House would soon be in place. The vision tarried, for five years. These were difficult years for Anne and the Matthew House Board.

At first they partnered with a small church that recently purchased an old YWCA building that had space for a potential refugee shelter. The building was too large for the small church and needed a lot of work. The Matthew House Board agreed to share the space, help with the renovations and pay some rent. Their excitement over these new possibilities came to a swift end when the local neighbourhood residents, most of them immigrants, raised zoning issues. They didn't want refugees in the neighbourhood. The local City Councilman called a neighbourhood meeting to discuss the issue. The meeting was horrible, Anne remembers. Local residents yelled, "We don't want any refugees! Nobody helped us when we got to Canada!" She felt it helped her understand what Jesus went through as he faced the angry mob before his crucifixion. This tense debate continued for over a year until the Councilman finally dropped the issue, leaving them free to pursue their efforts.

Finally, it seemed that God had prevailed and a permanent Matthew House would soon be a reality in the building with that small church. Again hopes soared. They developed a proposed architectural design for renovations. In that process, however, they discovered that to bring the space up to city fire codes, it would cost $150,000, which they did not have. The joint project with the small church died.

With no other alternatives they began looking for places to rent. They found several potential properties, but every time they mentioned refugees they got the same response. "You're not putting refugees in my house." During that time, Christine Martin told Anne of an agency called CityHome, a city housing organization that rented houses owned by the city. Anne wrote CityHome a hand-written letter fully explaining their need. "I was open and explicit," she said, knowing that the mention of refugees would probably cause them to turn us down.

By this time, the CBOQ had raised enough funds for her to quit her job at the community shelter and work full-time to start a Matthew House. On the surface, this appeared to be a very positive development. However, Anne found herself in a very lonely place. She no longer had co-workers to encourage her every day. She dealt with the failures of her work alone. During this same period, she had some potentially serious health issues, a family member passed away and she experienced other personal challenges. Anne entered a low place in her life. She was discouraged and ready to give up. As she looks back on those days, she can now philosophically remark, "Sometimes there is a battle before the victory."

We wonder sometimes why the vision God places in our lives takes so long to materialize and it's difficult not to get impatient or give up. Perhaps, we start second-guessing ourselves. "Is this really something I can do? Is this really what God wants to happen or is it just somehow my personal dream?" It wasn't God's plan for Matthew House to share the old YWCA building. It didn't seem to be God's plan to find a house to rent either.

Henry Blackaby's book, Experiencing God, became an important encouragement to Anne in those dark days. She kept returning to one of the things Blackaby wrote: "The world is yet to see what God can do through one man or woman who is fully committed to him." She wanted to be that woman. She told me, "I just wanted to walk with God and join God in what he was doing. God was at work, but, oh, life was hard."

Later, during a quiet time on retreat, Anne asked God over and over, "Do you really want me to start a house? Do you really want a house?" God's "yes" did not come. Neither did a "no." Instead, God seemed to be saying, "Anne, house or no house, what I really want is for you to know me and to walk with me." Tears filled Anne's eyes in the retelling of this moment. "I thought to myself," she said, "that's what I want. I just want to walk with God." It was a critical moment of trust and faith that ultimately placed all her dreams in God's hands. We can spend our time pursuing God's vision as if it's ours alone rather than understanding that ultimately it's God's vision. When we walk in faith, God will provide every answer.

On returning home from the retreat, Anne prayed with her roommate and relinquished the vision, the whole idea of the Matthew House, to God. She said, "Lord, Matthew House or no Matthew House, I just want to know you. I just want to walk with you." Tears flowed as she remembered her prayer, she dabbed at her eyes with a tissue. "Whatever I do, Lord, I just want you to be glorified." This is the irony and the power of faith. When we work and fret over what needs to be done and try to find answers, we often fail. When we come to the point of relinquishing it all back to God and realize we can do nothing on our own, God works miracles beyond what we could ever do alone.

Soon after her moment of relinquishment, Anne received word from Ross at CityHome that they had a house on Dundas Street West in Toronto that was available to rent for their purposes. He said, "It's been recently renovated, has six bedrooms, and backs onto a park. When she and other Board members went to look at it, they knew it was perfect. They were excited and filled with praise. Little did they know that this euphoria was once again about to evaporate.

Ross called again, "Anne, I have some terrible news for you. The City of Toronto is in the process of amalgamating all the municipalities into one metropolitan area. As a result of these negotiations and structural changes, all the rental properties owned by the city are frozen until further studies are done. The Dundas house is on that list," he said.

"No!" Anne said. "It's such an ideal house. Any idea how long this will take?"

"Oh, Anne, this could take years knowing how our bureaucracy works," Ross replied. "You might as well forget about it."

Anne could not understand. She thought for sure this house was what God wanted for them. She asked God, "Why? Why?" Then she remembered a prayer she had been praying based on what she was learning from Henry Blackaby. "Lord, I want you to do things that only God can do." This was one of those situations. If this house was to be theirs, only God could make it happen.

A couple of days after the bad news, the team gathered at the home of Christine Martin who lived only a few blocks from the Dundas Street house. Some doubted their dream would ever materialize. Others wanted to talk about what plans B and C might look like. Karen, one of their members and a woman of great faith, said "Wait a minute. Let's not give up. Let's keep praying. If God really wants us to have this house he will make a way." Anne wanted to believe her. She wanted to believe in the power of God. Since they were so close to the potential house and no one was living in it they all walked over to Dundas Street. They entered the back yard and laid hands on the house. "Lord," they prayed, "You hold the hearts of kings in the palm of your hand. Your Word says that. We pray that somehow you will break through city bureaucracy and red tape and that you will somehow release this house for our purposes—soon." I love the ending of that prayer because it's what I find myself praying all the time. "Soon, Lord, please." This small group of believers had been waiting five years. How much longer would it have to go on?

Very soon, after this prayer of faith, Anne got a message to call CityHome. When she did, the secretary asked, "Are you still interested in that house on Dundas Street West?

"Yes!" Anne replied.

"When would you like to move in?"

"How about next month?"

It was done. When they went down to sign the lease they talked to Ross personally. "Ross, what happened? How did the city lift its rental freeze?" they asked.

"Actually, they didn't lift it," he said. "The rental freeze is still on. I can't explain it. For some reason I simply could not get that house out of my mind so I finally went to the powers that be and explained your purposes to them. I asked for an exception that could be made just for this house. It was granted."

Although Ross couldn't explain it, Anne could. This was something only God could do. It was the final exclamation mark on the power of God and the rightness of this house for their Matthew House purposes.

THE FIRST YEARS

Within a month they moved in. The day after they opened, they were full. Although Anne and her Board had no doubt that God was with them, they still had bills to pay, volunteers to enlist and details to work out. They had little funding. Anne was the only staff member. They needed to pay the first month's rent and buy food. She remembered many verses in the Old and New Testaments in which God provided for the alien and the stranger. So she prayed, "Lord, if you are in this we know you will provide." A Presbyterian church two hours away from Toronto had a refugee fund they were ready to close. By God's grace they heard about the new Matthew House and gave them $4000 from the fund—enough to cover first and last months' rent. The national Baptist organization of Canada, Canadian Baptists Ministries (CBM) paid a third of Anne's salary that year; the Baptist Women of Ontario and Quebec (BWOQ) paid the rest. God was in this; God did provide.

About nine months before the Matthew House opened, during her dark days, Anne met with John and Amy Derrick, a couple from the Cooperative Baptist Fellowship (CBF) in the United States. They came to Canada to do a study on possible mission sites in North America that were related to internationals. Over dinner, Anne told them her vision. They took notes, thanked Anne for her help and returned to the United States. Anne thought little more about them.

As the Matthew House's August opening date approached, Anne felt the pressure, the needs and the responsibility. She enlisted a couple to be house parents, but she knew that was not going to be enough. She was becoming overwhelmed with the pressure, the needs, and the responsibility. Anne confided her anxiety to Sandy, a close friend. "I need help," she said.

"Let's just pray," Sandy said, and she did. "Lord, Anne needs help. Please send her labourers."

Soon afterwards Anne received a call from the Derricks who had visited her from CBF. "We finished our report," they said. "We really liked the possibilities in Toronto. It just happens that there is a couple, Marc and Kim Wyatt, who have recently returned from Thailand. They have a few years left on their service. Would you mind if they came up and worked with you?"

"Would I mind?" Anne said. "I would love it!"

The Wyatts moved to Toronto within a week of the Matthew House official opening in August 1998. They hit the ground running. With funds from CBF, Marc purchased a van they used to gather used furniture and move hundreds of refugee families into apartments following their stay at Matthew House. He worked closely with the leadership of the CBOQ and their umbrella organization, the Canadian Baptist Ministries (CBM). Kim helped cook meals and befriend the people who came through the house. Not long after, Clarence and Nancy Webb joined the team. Clarence, who eventually became treasurer, was a retired school teacher. Nancy was the Director of the Baptist Women of Ontario and Quebec. Nancy and Kim joined forces to get information out to the Baptist women across the province.

Again, God heard the prayers of his faithful servants and provided the labourers they needed to make Matthew House possible. Although everything was not easy or perfect in the early years, those involved knew they were walking and ministering in the will of God.

EXPANSION

Since Matthew House opened in August 1998, Anne and her staff have welcomed over 1000 refugee claimants from 84 countries. Those who walk through her doors are doctors, lawyers, professors and engineers, to name some of the professional people that have had to flee their country. Matthew House welcomes those who are well educated and those who are illiterate in the name of Jesus. One thing refugees share in common is the flight from persecution and need for a safe place to call home.

The Matthew House staff and volunteers offer a safe loving family-like environment, provide the necessary legal counsel, accompany them to refugee hearings and help them find and furnish an apartment. In short, they do all they can to help refugee claimants get settled in Canada. Anne says, "I have come to realize that we are not just a stop gap along the way, but we are an ongoing community for many; in some cases, we remain family for those who have none."

Typically, refugees stay in Matthew House for six to eight weeks before they find their own apartment and move out. Over the years, however, the staff realized that some refugees are not ready to move out on their own that quickly. They have dealt with too much trauma, have fewer adaptive skills for their new country, or are really young (unaccompanied minors) and vulnerable and have difficulty adjusting. As a result, Anne and her staff began to dream of a longer term home where these refugees could move as a next step to their eventual independence.

As always, they began with prayer. "Lord you know our need; how will we fill it?" World Vision was willing to give them funding for a transition staff person, but they needed another house. Once again, God showed his favour and did what only God could do. Anne received a phone call from a couple at one of the churches where she had spoken. Although they had never supported Matthew House before, they came for a visit and heard the vision for an additional house. They told Anne, "You go house hunting. When you find a house, let us know." When they found an ideal house on Shirley Street they informed the couple of the price. That couple wrote a cheque for the full amount. In 2011, a third house was added. This same couple paid half the cost.

When I asked Anne what her future vision for Matthew House was, her first response was "A Center of Hope at the end of the Refugee Highway." But her vision is larger than a single welcoming place for refugee claimants in Toronto. She dreams of a global network of Matthew Houses all along the Refugee Highway. The Board's stated vision is, "Matthew House envisions a vast network of Christian communities beginning in Canada and stretching around the world, capable of welcoming and assisting all refugees in their journey from risk and danger to safety and security." This is audacious. It's bold. It's beyond anything she or anyone else can do alone, but as Anne's ministry has shown us, nothing is impossible with God.

Faces seen at Matthew House Toronto.

Beds for Children

There is a passage in Acts 17—the one in which Paul is talking about the unknown God. He says, "This god determined the time set for us and the exact places we should live." So many times through my work with refugees I've seen God's exact timing. That first summer when we had our pilot project, it was a rainy night in July and I was sitting in a small office in the basement of a church office building. A volunteer brought in a little rollaway bed that had been donated. Then a former resident from Afghanistan came and returned a portable baby bed. Someone had given them a crib and they no longer needed the portable bed.

Half an hour later I got a call out of the blue. I learned there were Kurdish Iraqis at the bus station looking for a place to stay. Could we take them? It was a husband, wife, two children and a single man. I looked at our roster and decided we had room so I said okay. About 30 minutes later the doorbell rang and there were two men. The wife and children were still at the bus station. I showed the husband two rooms where they could stay—the husband and wife in one room and the children in another. He said, "Our children are small and we would really like for them to stay in the same room with us. Do you have some small beds we could put them in?" I asked him what their ages are. He said, "Four years old and 14 months old." I thought to myself, "Those beds! They are the exact sizes we need. Lord you knew they were coming!"

Before I started working in this ministry, I would see refugees on TV walking down the highway carrying their belongings in fear and total destitution, and I would think, "God, did you lose control of the world over there? Are you really in control?" Now, having worked for the years I've worked, having seen how he sends two little beds for Iraqi-Kurdish children, I'm convinced he knows who's going to come through the door. I believe very much in John 3:16 that God does love the whole world.

Anne Woolger

An Evening at Matthew House

While visiting Matthew House Toronto, my wife and I had the privilege of sharing a meal with the house residents. We sat shoulder to shoulder around a large round table in their beautiful dining room. Dishes, lovingly prepared by volunteers, were passed around family style and each person helped himself or herself. These residents were from Central America, Africa and Iran. Some sat quietly unsure of their ability to communicate. Others talked freely of their day, of current Canadian politics and of the funny things happened to them since coming to Canada. They joked and laughed together. Despite the fact that they came from different cultures and from different situations, regardless of the language barriers, they shared the commonality of their home as if they had known each other all their lives, as if they were family.

That evening, after the meal, they came back and gathered around the communal table for a house meeting that Anne Woolger facilitated. She asked the questions, "If you come back to Matthew House in 10 years, what will your life look like? What kind of job will you have? What will your family be like? And how many children will you have?" In a subtle but effective way, Anne was moving their thoughts from the past to the possibilities of their new futures.

One at a time, the residents took turns sharing their dreams. Some wanted to get their High School diploma. Others saw themselves graduating from the university or opening their own business. Most saw themselves with families and happily settled in a safe home. I couldn't help think of the dramatic change that must have already taken place in the lives of these refugees. Just months or even weeks before, these individuals had few dreams other than to stay alive and protect their family.

Joey Clifton

CHAPTER **3**

MATTHEW HOUSE FT. ERIE

Jim McNair

In 1999, First Baptist Church in Ft. Erie, Ontario was maintaining the status quo with a regular attendance of about 75 people—the number it had been for years. In 2002 they suspended their Sunday school for lack of attendance and put on hold a remodelling project. There were few young families and no babies in the congregation. Since that time, however, First Baptist has more than doubled in size. In 2006 they built an addition that included an elevator, more seating, a larger nursery to hold more than 10 babies on most Sundays and added more Sunday School classrooms.

The Sunday my wife and I visited First Baptist we participated in an adult Bible study class led by Adrien Wilsonne, the church's Associate Pastor, and a refugee from Haiti. He taught in English but occasionally moved to French to help some of the other Haitian members understand what he was saying. The class also included some long time local members and others from around the world.

At the worship hour the sanctuary filled with the colours of the world. In front of me, an active Asian preschooler kept turning around to show me his beautiful smile. An exotic looking African woman with three daughters slipped into the back. Another African woman raised her hands in praise during the music, her husband keeping rhythm on the drums at the front of the sanctuary. Two boys from Columbia stood in the aisle at the back so they could see what was happening on the platform. A quartet of teenagers from different parts of the world sang a song of dedication to Pastor Gary Page and his wife who were retiring that day. During the children's time, a multi-cultural assembly of children filled the platform.

After the worship service everyone packed into the downstairs fellowship hall for a celebratory dinner. Asians and North Americans embraced. Africans and Central Americans laughed and shared food together. These were scenes I had never witnessed before, involving so many people. It reminded me of Jesus' words in Mark's account of the temple cleansing. That day, Jesus reminded those who were misusing his house that it was intended to be a "house of prayer for all nations." First Baptist Church, Ft. Erie, truly is a house of prayer for all nations.

In my experience, most churches are homogeneous. That is, members have similar backgrounds, ethnicities and socioeconomic status. For the most part, we like it that way. Worship experiences are predictable. We can remember and pronounce everyone's name correctly. We bring similar expectations about worship styles and the administration of programs. When First Baptist began reaching out to refugees at their doorstep, some long-time members found it uncomfortable. Some of these people eventually left the church. Others began to see the wondrous beauty of the change and chose not only to accept it, but to embrace it as God's doing. The new members brought them stories of deep faith. They brought gifts and insights. They brought vitality and hope.

CATCHING THE VISION

The flood of new members started with one, then another and another. Slowly, refugees coming across the border at Ft. Erie began to find their way to First Baptist Church. The congregation heard of Anne Woolger's ministry to refugees in Toronto and invited her to come speak in December 1999. Before the morning worship service Anne told the pastor, "I can't just speak about Matthew House Toronto. With you being right on the border, I can't resist but challenge your congregation to open their own Matthew House." His response was affirming, "Anne, do whatever the Holy spirit is leading you to do." So Anne prayed, "Lord, I'm not here to force anyone to do anything. I'm just here to see who you're preparing and what you're doing."

Then she spoke. She told them there were 8000 refugees coming across their border every year and there was a shortage of space. At that time Casa el Norte was the only shelter in Ft. Erie. It had eight beds. Anne shared stories of refugees and challenged them to open their own Matthew House in Ft. Erie. After the service, she met with a Bible study class of about 20 people. They asked many questions about how to start a Matthew House.

Shirley Ann Morrison was one of those in attendance that day who was moved by Anne's words. "She was talking about Matthew House Toronto and I'm thinking we have these people. They are coming. We have to do this. It was the Holy Spirit." While telling this to me Shirley Ann's eyes filled with tears. The clear call of God's Spirit within her and the clear call of God for her church overwhelmed her.

After Anne's visit, First Baptist immediately formed a steering committee chaired by Jim McNair to explore the need and look into the possibility of opening a Matthew House ministry. The committee met weekly. A small group of them traveled to Toronto to learn more about the Matthew House there. Before long, the church decided to transform their vacant parsonage, located half a block away from the church, into a Matthew House.

The Anglicans, Catholics, and Lutherans that ran Casa el Norte applied for a $5000 grant to help First Baptist. Jim McNair filled out a Launching Pad Grant application of-

At First Baptist Church, Ft. Erie.

fered by the Canadian Baptists of Ontario and Quebec (CBOQ). They hammered out by-laws, formed a Board and hired a director who set up the office and visited other shelters to learn what she could about running a house for refugees. October 15, 2000 was the targeted opening date, only ten months after Anne Woolger's challenge. On October 13, they received a request from Canada Immigration to provide shelter for three newly arrived Buddhist Monks from Tibet. Within a few days the ministry of Matthew House was in full swing with guests from Tibet, Congo, Nigeria and Russia.

Only ten months passed from the time Anne challenged them to the opening of Matthew House Ft. Erie. Yes, a great deal of work took place in those ten months, but it is clear that when God's people come together with a common God-inspired vision, much can be accomplished.

Since that time, close to 1500 refugees have come through Matthew House Ft. Erie. Jim McNair, now the Ministry Coordinator at the House, asked a former guest, "What was the most important thing we were able to give to you?" her answer came back, "Hope." They restore hope in the lives of people who have lost it. Jim confesses, "We get up every morning wondering how God is going to surprise us in this new day."

CHAMPIONS

The first director First Baptist hired for their new Matthew House didn't stay long. When she left, Shirley McNair and Eva Gutbrod stepped in as the interim directors. They discovered that they loved it. After a year, Eva joined her husband, also named Jim, on a mission trip to Africa and Shirley became the full-time house manager. Jim McNair supports her day-to-day administration of the house as Ministry Coordinator. Together, they are the champions of the Matthew House in Ft. Erie. Every house needs a champion or two—people who are devoted to making it work, seeking partners, finding solutions, organizing volunteers and spending much time in prayer.

When my wife and I arrived at Jim and Shirley's home as part of this project, he took a while to come to the door. He'd been on a ladder on his back porch wrestling with an awning. I could tell immediately that Jim was an active retiree, unafraid to get his hands dirty or tackle any project. Although he and Shirley are retired school teachers, they are far from inactive. They are now missionaries in their own home town.

In order to help refugee claimants find Matthew House, Jim and Shirley needed to build solid relationships with key partners in the area—Canada Immigration, the Multi-Cultural Center, immigration lawyers, and others. They worked with a network of non-governmental organizations and Canada Immigration to develop a refugee processing unit called the Peace Bridge Newcomers Welcome Centre, the only one in Canada. There, refugee claimants find a place to relax and receive welcome from specially trained officers as they await the sometimes lengthy process of getting into the country.

Jim, Shirley, Rosemary Legge (a faithful co-worker) and others provide the house residents with their immediate needs, give assistance with immigration procedures, provide transportation, assist with forms, help overcome language barriers, orient new comers to Canadian life and offer encouragement. When the refugee claimants are ready to move out of Matthew House, Jim and Shirley help them find suitable lodging and help them find furniture from their furniture warehouse that is stocked through donations. Ten years before Matthew house got started, the government housing facility was full of drugs and crime. Now, these same housing units are filled with refugees, many of whom came through Matthew House. It is a safer, friendlier place to live.

Getting started in a new country is a difficult task. Refugees need ongoing support, which Jim offers through their Aftercare Ministry. He helps people connect with schools, job and health care providers. He helps them understand mail and bills that need to be paid. He even teaches them to drive, gives advice on vehicle purchases and advocates for them with numerous agencies. Asrat, a former Matthew House resident, said that Shirley and Jim are more like parents. They work so hard. "Sometimes," she told me, "Jim just shows up at my house with something new. Once he brought me a TV stand that matches my furniture. They fill everyone's house with joyful gifts. They build life."

PARTNERS

Despite the key leadership role that Jim and Shirley play, the success of a Matthew House can never be about one or two people. Champions need many others to come alongside them. From the beginning, the members of First Baptist Church supported the ministry by offering the parsonage without charge. They paid the utilities and phone bills. When the larger house next door to the church became available, the church sold the parsonage. The proceeds provided a small loan to enable the Matthew House Board to get a mortgage for the purchase of the more suitable home.

Not long after First Baptist launched the Matthew House ministry, the steering committee invited other Baptist churches in the Association to join them. As Christians from other local churches heard about the ministry, they added their support as well. At this point, the governing Board includes members from several denominations. Volunteers from churches represent a variety of faith traditions and they help with numerous tasks every week.

During those early days, Marc and Kim Wyatt, Cooperative Baptist Fellowship (CBF) workers living in Toronto, came to Ft. Erie several times to give support and encouragement. When a group of Cooperative Baptists from Virginia happened to be visiting Toronto, Laurie Barber encouraged them to stop by Matthew House, Ft. Erie. That visit led to other mission visits by several couples and young people from CBF churches, particularly from the Richmond, Virginia area.

Every summer since 2004 Stu and Eleanor Dodson from First Baptist Church, Richmond make the trip north to Ft. Erie. They stay a month to repair things, scrub floors, sort clothing, talk to guests, befriend people and give Jim and Shirley the summer break that they need. When telling me about this couple, Jim says, "They are a blessing."

The blessing goes both directions. Stu and Eleanor find great blessing in their giving. They describe Matthew House as a heart ministry. "It's just about loving people," Eleanor said. "We give them hugs and take them into our lives every day." She remembers one particular conversation she had with a woman from Ghana who was given away by her family and forced into servitude at age six. Twenty five years later she escaped. After a long journey, she found herself at Matthew House. At one point, she told Eleanor her story. Eleanor told her, "Your faith is strong. You know, I love you and Jesus loves you too." With those words, the woman began to cry. "Do you know that no one ever told me they loved me until I came to Matthew House?" the woman said, "I never heard the word love in my whole life."

Shirley McNair (top left) and other faces seen at Matthew House Ft. Erie.

God is Here

Dominic didn't stay at Matthew House, Ft. Erie when she crossed the border into Canada, but that didn't matter. She still considers it her home. When the situation in Haiti became unbearable, she fled to the United States to be with family and friends. When that didn't work out, she returned to Haiti only to find things had not changed and she was still in great danger. Eventually, she contacted a friend in Canada who helped her navigate her way across the border.

She initially stayed in a temporary shelter for refugees in Buffalo, New York for 12 days. It was a difficult and frustrating time for her. "I remember my grandmother always says, 'There is no resurrection without death.' So I thought to myself maybe this is the death part." Once across the border, Dominic found her way to a shelter not far from First Baptist Church where she began attending worship services. Immediately, Jim and Shirley McNair adopted her. Today, Dominic refers to them as her dad and mom. When she first arrived in Canada she talked to her father back in Haiti who was worried about her. She told him, "God gave me a family here."

Following her arrival in Canada, Dominique came to understand the love of Christ in a new way. She says, "When I saw the way people are so helpful and so lovely, I said, 'God is working there.' If people can be like this, God is here."

Dominic

I Cried. I Cried. I Cried.

John has four daughters living in Zimbabwe that he hasn't seen in the 15 years since he fled his country. He was working for a struggling company that was purchased through deceptive means by one of President Mugabe's cousins. The new owner fired the personnel manager, the accountant, and the general manager, then took control of the finances of the company. He took money from employees' paychecks.

All along John and other employees thought the withholdings from their paychecks were going to pay their income tax, contributing to their pensions and paying for their medical aid. At the end of the year, the government claimed they didn't have any of the tax that was due. Others who went to doctors discovered they had no medical aid available. Their pensions had been wiped out as well. When the employees hired a lawyer to fight the injustice, President Mugabe gave a presidential order that prevented any action against his cousin.

"We lost out on everything," John said. Many became homeless. Those who continued to oppose the government's action were beaten or imprisoned.

John fled to the United States where he tried to make a new life. The process for refugee claimants in the United States is very murky and dangerous. No one knows how to go about it. First, most refugees are afraid. They come from a frightening place and don't know what to expect from the U.S. police. In John's case the police in Zimbabwe used to torture and beat people. When the ruling party beat him, he could not report it to the police because the police would do the same thing.

Second, because they cannot ask for help from the police who might arrest them for being illegal refugees, they seek help from people who take advantage of their ignorance and make them victims. John listened to false advice and acquired a fake social security card that he did not know was falsified. As soon as he discovered it, he reapplied correctly and was granted a legitimate card.

After six years of working, gaining promotions and finding a new life in the United States, the falsified social security card caught up with him. He was arrested, fined $1500 and imprisoned for 12 months. "I cried. I cried. I cried. Oh goodness, I cried," he said. "I ran away from Zimbabwe's prisons and here I am again in prison. I didn't intend to do this."

John

When the time came for John's hearing to officially immigrate to the United States, he was denied admittance and forced to leave. Today, John lives in Canada where he has made his new home. He may never see his daughters again.

It Felt Like Home

Patience was the first person from Zimbabwe to come to Matthew House, Ft. Erie. She was 16 years old and alone. Her father had been the manager of a farm that was confiscated illegally by so-called friends of the government. When the new owners approached him about continuing to manage the farm, he told them, "No. It's not really your farm." As a result, the new owners forced Patience's family to leave the farm and move to the city where things were in chaos. Gangs of young men were beating people, particularly family members of those who weren't doing what the government wanted them to do. Patience's life was in danger, so her parents sent her to Canada.

When she first arrived she didn't know anyone and she was afraid. On arriving at Matthew House, however, it felt like home. She sat down with Jim and Shirley McNair and had some chicken soup. Then she and another young refugee who had just arrived went on a walk down to the river, something she could not have safely done in Zimbabwe. They stood looking at the water for a while. Finally, Patience said, "I'm okay." Her new friend responded, "I'm okay, too."

Patience received her Canadian citizenship on Canada Day in 2009. She graduated High School and college. Today she is at the university furthering her studies. She describes those six years between 2003 when she arrived and the moment she received her citizenship as difficult years. "Sometimes it feels like you're going through life without knowing what tomorrow brings. It's like you almost have to live in your suitcase kind of feeling." Refugees live with a great deal of anxiety about their future and whether or not they will ever see their families again. Their lives are on hold until their claim is finalized.

After Patience became a Canadian citizen she returned to Zimbabwe to see her family. Although she was thrilled to see her parents and brothers again, life there is still tense and uncertain. She is happy with her new home in Canada.

Patience

God is in Charge

Adrien was a popular man in Haiti. He was a university teacher and a pastor. Many of his students and friends encouraged him to run for political office. This, indeed, was his intention when three men stopped him on his way home one evening. One of the men grabbed his motorcycle and put a gun to his ear. They insulted him, cursed him, and threatened to kill him. He took it seriously and left for Canada.

When immigration told him about Matthew House next to a church, he decided to stay in Ft. Erie rather than to go to Montreal where there was a French speaking Haitian community. The transition for Adrien and his family was difficult in many ways. His three-year-old son didn't speak the language and could not communicate, but he was blessed with a day-care teacher who loved him. His teen-age children could speak English, but they missed their friends and other school children didn't talk to them.

For Adrien, the adjustment was perhaps even more difficult. "When you first come," he said, "you were someone back home. You were doing something. You were an active citizen. You had a job; you had a home; you had everything. Here you start from scratch. You go from the top to the bottom." When Adrien was in Haiti, he felt self-sufficient. He took care of himself and others. People relied on him, and he relied on himself. When he came to Canada, though, he says, "I didn't have anything in me. I felt I lost part of my self-esteem."

This extremely frustrating and humbling experience, however, proved to be a time of great faith building for Adrien. He discovered he could no longer rely on himself. Instead, he had to rely on God. He prayed, "Lord, I have no fame. I rely on you. Take my hand and lead me where you want me to be. I know you have the best thing for me. Just open my eyes so I can see." God said, "Don't worry Adrien. I am taking you somewhere."

Today, Adrien is Associate pastor of First Baptist Church, Ft. Erie, a position he would not have imagined a few years ago. He is positive that God is in charge of his life. He says, "I don't know what is going to happen next, but I know God is with me. He is leading me. "

Adrien

CHAPTER **4**

MATTHEW HOUSE WINDSOR

Joanne King

Joanne King called it her Moses Experience. She was head of the Baptist Women at Grace Baptist in Windsor. Her church, along with others in the Association, was talking about starting a Matthew House like the one in Toronto. In the fall of 1999, Anne Woolger came to visit and shared her vision at a meeting with local pastors. In April of the next year she spoke at Grace Baptist on Baptist Women's Sunday. She spoke on the topic, "The World at Our Border and on Our Doorstep." Stan Mantle, the pastor said, "Anne hit us with a double-barrelled shot from the Old and the New Testament."

When foreigners reside among you in your land, do not mistreat them. The foreigners residing among you must be treated as your native-born. Love them as yourself, for you were foreigners in Egypt. I am the Lord your God. (Lev. 19:33-34)

Keep on loving one another as brothers and sisters. Do not forget to show hospitality to strangers, for by so doing some people have shown hospitality to angels without knowing it. Continue to remember those in prison as if you were together with them in prison, and those who are mistreated as if you yourselves were suffering. (Hebrews 13:1-3)

Afterwards, Anne and Joanne went for a walk. God was moving in Joanne's life. She asked Anne, "What else would it take to open a Matthew House here?"

In May and June additional meetings were held with other local CBOQ churches to talk about the idea of a Matthew House in Windsor. At the end of the June meeting it was clear that if the venture was going to proceed someone needed to step forward as leader, but no one did. In September, Joanne met with Stan Mantle to ask him what was happening with the refugee ministry. "Nothing," he said. No one stepped forward to lead it. With a great deal of fear and trepidation, Joanne said she would help and that she was being led in that direction. She still refers to it as her Moses Experience because "I kept bringing up reasons why it shouldn't be me." She admits she didn't know anything about refugee ministry other than what she had heard at the meetings. But she was a recently retired elementary school teacher with a willing heart.

Ultimately, what God requires from any of us is a willing heart—a desire to listen to the Holy Spirit's guidance in our life and the courage to be obedient. Joanne wasn't going to lead the Israelite refugees out of slavery and oppression into a new land, but she was going to lead in the effort to offer welcome to whatever refugees found their way to her land. She admits that at the beginning she was clueless. "I didn't know the difference between a sponsored refugee and a refugee claimant." We often enter ministry with ignorance and uncertainty. Perhaps that is exactly where God wants us because then we learn to rely on Him. We begin with humility and deep desire to learn.

PREPARATION

Joanne began by contacting churches to let them know about the vision for a Matthew House in Windsor. She visited the Matthew House in Toronto. She visited agencies in Windsor who already worked with refugees in order to determine what the needs were, specifically whether or not there was need for shelter. Sister Helen from the Windsor Refugee Office was particularly helpful to Joanne and aided her in making numerous connections. In October, 2000, Sister Helen met with interested individuals at First Baptist Church and cleared up many of their concerns. In December, she came to Grace Baptist for a Wednesday evening presentation and brought refugees with her.

An Albanian girl told about her experience of coming to Windsor and not having a place to stay. Joanne remembers her saying, "If you people can do this thing it would be wonderful." There was a sense among the small group who came that evening that they were being called to do this.

In January, 2001, eleven people representing five CBOQ churches met with Anne Woolger at Grace Baptist. That evening, eight people came forward to establish a steering committee. In February they met again at First Baptist with Ron Watson, a CBOQ Area Minister and Joanne King was elected Chair. They also agreed to apply for a launching grant from the Missional Initiatives division of CBOQ. This division helps facilitate partnerships, offers missions' training and provides grants for mission initiatives to its own churches.

Over the next year, the planning group received support from the Western Association of Baptist Churches, applied for the CBOQ grant funds, began the process of incorporation and sought a CBOQ mortgage for purchasing a house. They also spent the year seeking other funding. Their first donation came from the Essex United Church of Christ in Windsor. Cooperative Baptist Fellowship agreed to a future $5000 donation to the Baptist Women, once the house was in full operation.

The CBOQ approved the Launching grant in early 2002. In addition, CBOQ agreed to hold the mortgage but ministry organizers had to raise a percentage of the loan. CBOQ provided $40,000 worth of investment certificates that individuals and Grace Baptist purchased. The money came in quickly. By July, their organization was incorporated as the Windsor

Baptist Refugee Ministries and their Steering Committee became a Board of Directors. Excitement was high.

The Board closed on the sale of their house on Drouillard Road at the end of August and took possession in September. The home was far from ready for refugees so renovations began. A partial wall was removed on the main floor. New cupboards were put in and an overhaul of half the basement took place. All along the way individuals gave donations for these special projects. By January, 2003 the house was ready to open. Then disaster struck.

Joanne recalls that it was a cold January morning and she was out of town. She received a call from someone at her church who had just received a call from a woman living across the street from the new house.

"Are you the church who bought the house?" she said to the man at the church.
"Yes we are," he replied.

"Well, I think you have a problem."

The description Joanne received over the phone was that water was pouring out of the basement windows. A burst pipe in the downstairs bathroom was gushing water. They began the clean up and restoration. They pumped out the water, hauled everything out and started over. This time, they renovated the entire basement with the donations that kept coming in. Finally, a small staff was in place by March, 2003 and they were ready to begin.

It took them almost four years from Anne Woolger's first challenge to the point where they were ready to open the doors. It took commitment and tireless effort. It took partners and cooperation. It took persistence and faith, but they did not give up even through disaster and setbacks. Joanne told me this story over dinner in her home. Others who were present, such as Stan and Heather Mantle, reminisced together. They laughed at their ignorance and false starts. They bemoaned the difficulties. They continued to be amazed at how God worked things out, how others joined the vision and how exciting it was to be working within the will of God.

As I listened to their stories, I wondered if I would have given up. Is it really worth all this effort? Will we ever see the fruit of our labours? Does God really want us to do this? Surely, if he did, things would go more smoothly. God is in charge. Right? This should be simple. We often make the mistake of thinking that just because something is God's will, then it shouldn't be difficult. In reality, when God calls us to something important, Satan does everything possible to make it difficult, to cause problems and to discourage us so that we give up. Yet, if we stay the course like the faithful group in Windsor, God uses our struggles to teach us perseverance, character and hope:

But we also glory in our sufferings, because we know that suffering produces perseverance; perseverance, character; and character, hope. And hope does not put us to shame, because God's love has been poured out into our hearts through the Holy Spirit, who has been given to us. (Romans 5:3-5)

RESIDENTS AT LAST!

Matthew House Windsor's first resident, a young man from the Congo, arrived on April 1, 2003. He stayed only a few days before moving on to Toronto. It was a nice way to start. Next came a Muslim woman from Pakistan. While taking her around the city as part of her orientation, they passed Grace Baptist. Joanne said, "This is my church and it's one of the churches that supports Matthew House."
She responded with, "I want to come to church."

"It's a Baptist Church," Joanne said. "And you're Muslim."

"Yes, I know," she replied. She explained that when she was in Pakistan she always wanted to go in a church, but she couldn't in her country.

She came to the Good Friday Service that year. Afterwards she said, "I will never miss Good Friday." She hasn't. She comes sometimes on Sunday as well.
After one more family came, Joanne and the Board realized they didn't have enough staff because she was quickly becoming exhausted. They made the difficult decision to close temporarily on the first of May. They took some time to reassess what needed to be done and eventually hired a full-time director and a night staff person.   The House was reopened in September. Even after the re-start things were difficult at times. Occasionally they had no money. At other times, the beds were not filled.

Gradually word spread though. Joanne contacted the Freedom House in Detroit where many refugees stayed temporarily before crossing the bridge into Windsor. They made connections with the new Canadian Center and other agencies that work with refugees in Windsor. Today, because of word of mouth, many refugee claimants know they want to go to Matthew House before they leave Africa or Haiti—or from wherever else they are fleeing. Cab drivers know to take refugee claimants to Matthew House. One day, when a refugee lady found her way to the Matthew House, she said, "Is this the place that takes in refugees?"

With her broken English she explained to Joanne that someone had dropped her at a small shopping center not far from Grace Baptist. She was lost. She found help from a stranger in the parking lot. When the refugee explained her problem, the woman said, "I know just the place."

In 2008, following the loss of her job, Heather Mantle approached Joanne about volunteering. For Joanne, the timing was perfect, as God's time always is. She was ready to step down as director of Matthew House and God arranged for Heather to step in.

RIPPLING EFFECT

Although Matthew House Windsor is not large, almost 400 refugees from more than 40 countries have called it home in the past eight years. Each refugee is an individual with his or her own story. Some come with great sadness, others with much joy. Heather told of a very depressed Haitian woman who came to them with a baby and two-year-old child. Her husband had been put in detention in the United States and she didn't know if they were going to let him go or deport him to Haiti. Over the next 12 months she became quite ill from the stress of her situation. Finally, the United States released her husband and he joined her in Canada. From that day forward, she looked ten years younger. "To see that whole family back together again was amazing," Heather said.

One Burundian family had four small boys. The father and mother each had responsible jobs in their home country. When Joanne visited them one day in their tiny, cramped apartment, she couldn't help notice their smiles. "You are happy. Big smiles," she said.

"Joanne, you have no idea what it means at night to be able to lay down in peace and in a safe place," the husband responded.

Since the beginning of Matthew House Windsor, many internationals found their way to Grace Baptist. Pastor Stan Mantle explains:

Refugees are people on a journey, a people uprooted from their homes and culture, their language and routine. Dropped in a new country with time on their hands while they await a response to their refugee application, they may be open to new experiences, new ideas, and different answers. What they are definitely open to is genuine care and help. An invitation to come to church may be accepted. Once their need for shelter, rest and food are met, their hearts and souls seek to make sense of what has happened to them. Aware of the need for guidance and support, Divine help is welcome and church is a logical place to seek it.

Stan Mantle, pastor of Grace Baptist Church

Faith, bruised and shattered, long forgotten and trampled down, may come to life in the interlude of quiet and peace which Matthew House affords, and when it does, the spiritual food and drink of a caring church may be gratefully received.

In the mid-1990s Grace Baptist was a thriving church averaging 160 each Sunday. Their Sunday school hall was full from front to back at 9:45 a.m. each week. Over the next decade a slow decline left only 10 people in their opening Sunday school session. Worship attendance decreased to 120. Then the refugees started coming because of Matthew House. Sunday morning attendance shot up to around 180, the average age of the congregation decreased considerably and on any given Sunday you will find 75 active children and youth filling the Sunday school. Today their congregation is multi-cultural and multi-linguistic. Some of these refugees have joined the leadership team as deacons or teachers.

A transition of this kind is not always simple. It requires give and take, adjusting to new ideas and overcoming communication barriers. No doubt some of the long-time members were challenged and stretched by the changes around them. Through perseverance, they enjoy the wonderful blessing of the world at their door and the opportunity to entertain strangers in their midst.

ABANDONED ON A STREET

The man who helped me did not sit with me on the plane. He never told me his name or what would happen next. When we arrived at our destination and got off the plane he held onto my passport. I never saw it. When we got through immigration he took me downtown in a taxi and we got out together and I do not know what street I was on. At this time, I did not even know . . . the name Toronto, or the fact that I was even in Canada. He said, "Now you are safe." He walked down the road and I never saw him again.

I was so very confused and depressed. I considered following that man but was afraid to because from the very beginning, he made it clear that he did not want to get to know me or even have a conversation with me.

It was 7:00 p.m. and I found a charitable organization to try to get help. They told me they did not have room for me and that they only took men. From there I did not know where to go. I did not know anyone and I was in much fear. I despaired of life itself. Had I come all this way only to die on the street in a foreign land? About 10:00 p.m. I saw a restaurant near where I was walking. I was so exhausted. I lay down and slept on the sidewalk outside the restaurant.

The next day when they opened the restaurant, I approached the old man in that place. He gave me something to eat and he took me to his home. He and his wife were good to me. I slept there that night. The next day they brought me to a bus station and they paid for my bus ticket and told me to go to Windsor because there was less crime there. I did not know what Windsor was; I thought maybe it was a refugee camp.

When I arrived in Windsor, I asked someone where there was a shelter and she took me to one. But the man who I met there said he could not take me and instead he took me to the police station. Once again I was full of fear. I told the police everything, my whole story of escaping for my life from the Congo. They called the shelter again and a taxi came and took me back.

Because of the terrible situation I was in, they allowed me to stay one night but said I could not remain there. I felt alone and afraid. The next day a staff woman arrived. I told her my story and she told me that a new shelter had just opened in Windsor called Matthew House and it was just for refugees like me.

At Matthew House, I met a wonderful lady who welcomed me with a big smile. Julie Gammon is that lady. Finally I felt welcomed and safe. There I learned how to make a refugee claim. Day after day and week after week, I am getting to understand the meaning of life and feeling hope again. . . . I am so grateful!

Taken from **"Inside Matthew House"** newsletter, Christmas, 2003

Separated from My Children

A refugee story is private and often so horrific they don't want to relive it by telling to a complete stranger. This is why I was honored that Celestinne allowed me into her neat, clean kitchen to talk about her life. When I asked her if she felt comfortable sharing her story she replied in her broken English, "I try. So sad story." Indeed, it was.

When she began to speak her voice dropped to almost a whisper as if these are things that cannot be spoken aloud. Celestinne's husband worked in the diamond business in Congo, a tug-of-war prize sought by opposing factions. Despite his innocence, he was caught in the middle, and killed. The killers then came to Celestinne's home wanting to kill the rest of the family. They destroyed everything in the house and shot Celestinne. The rest of her family—her father, her brothers and her 12 children were unharmed.

Wounded and scared, she escaped to a Convent where the Sisters cared for her for a year. During that time she was unable to see her children. The youngest was taken to South Africa by Celestinne's mother. The others hid out with their grandfather. At the end of the year, the Sisters who protected her smuggled her out of the country into South Africa by dressing her as one of them. There she was reunited with her youngest daughter. She recalls how difficult it was to leave the rest of her children, but she had no choice. As I listened I could not imagine leaving my children in a dangerous place like the Congo with no way to help them.

When she came to Matthew House, Windsor she was frightened. "I was not comfortable. It was like I was in my own country so maybe someone can come and attack me or something like that." Joanne King assured her she was safe now. The Matthew House staff helped her with all the immigration and social services procedures. They enrolled her in English classes. More than that, Celestinne says, "They loved me, too. I was feeling comfortable but sad because of not seeing my children." In addition, when she arrived in Canada she was diagnosed with cancer and the Matthew House staff took care of her daughter while she was in the hospital.

Celestinne is now well, has her Canadian citizenship and is enrolled in college. She has worked tirelessly with the staff at Matthew House to get her children out of Congo. When I met Celestinne, after 5 years of separation, she was recently reunited with her 10 children and a nephew she is raising because his parents were killed.

When I said to her, "Your life has certainly changed over the last six or seven years" she broke down and cried. Large tears rolled down her cheeks. Again her voice dropped to a whisper as if now the moment was a holy one. "I'm so happy to see them (the children) because I was like between death and life." She went on to say, "Life is full of surprises. We have ups and downs sometimes. It is just good to know God. You believe in God, everything is going to be okay." Indeed everything is going to be okay. Since I interviewed Celestinne, she has been united with her last daughter and the family is rejoicing.

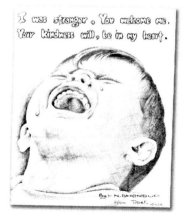

Drawing by a Tibetan monk who was one of the first refugees to stay at a Matthew House.

Getting to Know God

Susan arrived in Canada from Zimbabwe three years ago. She is an articulate bubbling ball of joy and laughter. When I interviewed her she talked fast with excitement as she relived her story. During the serious times, her voice slowed and dropped in volume. At the funny parts her voice rose with laughter. She switched back and forth between her characters as if she was replaying the scenes on stage.

Once she decided to go to Canada, she contacted Freedom House in Detroit to get help. They informed her they had no openings at the moment but she could stay in a nearby motel and they would make the appointment for her at the border. The morning of her appointment she called a cab to take her across the bridge. She knew she was only a few minutes from the bridge and the ride should not take long.

The cab driver said, "It will be $160."

"Really? To go to the bridge?" Susan asked.

"If you don't want to," he said, "you can find someone else."

She did not know anyone else, and she could not be late for the interview, so she accepted his terms. At the first barrier on the United States side, he demanded payment and refused to take her farther if she did not pay. Although the five minute drive cost her $160 she later found out that other Matthew House residents were victimized by such cab drivers for as much as $800.

Eventually Susan found her way to Matthew House where she had all her required paperwork and medical check-ups done within two weeks. She was anxious to get out on her own so she found a basement apartment. Heather Mantle, the director, said, "Oh, you don't need to move

out. You can stay a month."
Susan persisted, so Heather and
others helped her move into the
new apartment.

Not long afterwards, Susan
began experiencing terrible
headaches whenever she stayed
in her apartment all day. Heather
found another apartment for her,
but Susan had signed a six-
month lease. How was she
going to get out of it? Finally,

Susan and Heather Mantle

she decided to explain her problem to her landlord and try to get out of
the lease. She prayed, "God help me. Give me the words and show me
what I should do and how I should handle it."

Around 5:30 or 6:00 the next morning Susan got out of bed to use
the bathroom and stepped into a basement full of water. She said, "I just
started crying. I've just left Matthew House and starting fresh and what's
going to happen." She called the Landlord and Heather. Heather brought
Wayne, one of the volunteers. When they arrived, the landlord was vacu-
uming up the water with confidence that Susan would be back in her
apartment by nightfall.

They realized why Susan was having such headaches. This was ob-
viously not the first time this apartment had flooded. The apartment was
full of mold.

Wayne said, "She is not living here. She is moving out."

"She has a lease," the landlord said.

"Would you like me to call the Board of Health? Would you like me to call the city?" Wayne said.

The landlord let her out of the lease and returned her deposit check.

When Susan told Heather what she had prayed the night before, Heather said, "God didn't give you the words, but he answered your prayer."

Susan replied with, "Yeah sure. He has a sense of humor."

Susan had been mad at God for a long time, blaming him for all the difficult things she had endured in her life. She first visited Grace Baptist to appease a friend that invited her. It was the first time she had been in church for 10 years. The next Thursday she went to a women's Bible study. After that, she went every Sunday. She says, "My faith has grown a lot since I've been here. I've learned that I can't do anything on my own. I might think I can, but I can't. Also, when I'm going through really hard times I need to learn to depend on God because if I don't, it just makes the hard times worse. I think going through things sometimes helps you get to know God. If I had not gone through what I went through, I would have stayed at a comfortable place with God. I would not know him as he really is."

• • •

As I reflect on all the stories I've been told as I've worked on the Matthew House project, I realize that many refugees have greater faith than I do. They have experienced difficult circumstances that require them to place everything into the hands of God. We, who call ourselves the helpers, ministers, servants to these refugees, also must become their students.

Ambassador Bridge between Detroit and Windsor
where many refugees cross from the U.S. to Canada.

CHAPTER **5**

MATTHEW HOUSE MONTREAL

Christine Walsh

"I don't know what God is going to do because we are a work in progress. We're still figuring things out and putting things in place and seeing who God is going to bring along. It's really the Lord's project and we're just trying to keep up with him." These words of Christine Walsh, the Matthew House Montreal Director, represent the reality of following God's leadership. She and her ministry partner, Christopher Lu, entered their Matthew House ministry with a clear plan, but they have learned along the way that circumstances change. When they do, plans must change as well.

Many of us, and I include myself in this, like to have big projects like a Matthew House figured out in advance. We take time to think things through and write down each step so we will have a clear plan. Didn't Jesus teach us to plan ahead?

Suppose one of you wants to build a tower. Won't you first sit down and estimate the cost to see if you have enough money to complete it? For if you lay the foundation and are not able to finish it, everyone who sees it will ridicule you, saying, 'This person began to build and wasn't able to finish.' (Luke 14:28-30)

Then, of course, events occur that suddenly make our plan obsolete or at best, only partially workable. What do we do? Start all over? Give up? Trust that God will provide new plans? Even as we hear God's instructions to plan, we also hear Jesus' words in the Sermon on the Mount when he called on his followers to trust God with the future: "But seek first his kingdom and his righteousness, and all these things will be given to you as well. Therefore do not worry about tomorrow, for tomorrow will worry about itself. Each day has enough trouble of its own." (Matthew 6:33-34). Perhaps what God desires is exactly what Christine and Christopher have done—plan the best they can and trust the rest to God. When God is involved, we never know where the path may take us. Sometimes we're just along for the ride, which means giving up our need for control and trusting God for the details of tomorrow.

TWO STORIES CONVERGE

Christopher Lu is a Christian business man and member of the Montreal City West Baptist Church. In 1976, two years after North Vietnam took control of South Vietnam, he escaped among the boat people. After a year in an Indonesian refugee camp he came to Canada without his family. His first years were extremely difficult. Because of that experience, he understands the struggle of those coming to a new country with few supports and he has a heart to help them. "Being a refugee myself, I've experienced how difficult it is to settle in a land where people don't speak your language," he said. "I understand what it's like to live in a totally different country, helpless to find a job. I want to help them so they can stand on their own feet one day."

After Anne Woolger spoke at a Baptist Convention meeting in Montreal in 2002, Christopher had a long conversation with her. They discussed the idea of setting up a similar house in Montreal. He said, "If Matthew House had existed when I came as a refugee, life would have been different for me." Being the business person he is, Christopher began to plan for a Matthew House in Montreal, but he couldn't do it alone. He was missing someone to have the day-to-day contact with refugees coming into the city, someone to actually manage the house. He prayed for this ministry for seven years without giving up hope.

In the meantime God was preparing Christine Walsh for this very thing. Christine is a young adult who has always had a heart for service and ministry. As we sat at her dining room table talking about her journey she told me, "I had a lot of passion to help people, but I didn't know exactly how God wanted to use it." In search of her calling, she traveled to El Salvador, Guatemala, Trinidad and South Africa studying and doing mission work. But she kept being drawn back to Montreal, Canada's largest French-speaking city with 600,000 internationals from all over the world. "I felt constant assurance or conviction that God was going to call me back to Montreal."

On Christmas Eve, 2007, Christine searched the internet seeking ways she might be involved in ministry in Montreal and came across Matthew House Toronto's website. "I felt a strong stirring in my spirit," she said. "I wasn't sure if it was just emotion or really the Lord, but it stayed with me for months and months." Figuring out God's will and desire for our lives is often a difficult thing, but when such a stirring continues with us, God's Spirit is likely at work. Christine began praying about this Matthew House project and the burden for it that God laid on her heart. One of her prayers was "If this is really where you are leading me, lead me to other like-minded people."

Eventually, Christine went to Toronto where she spent three days helping Anne Woolger at Matthew House. She helped with their tenth anniversary celebration and translated the event for some French speaking residents. "It was just awesome. I felt like I was home, like I had always done this," she said. She returned to Montreal and continued to pray. While waiting, Christine began volunteering at the YMCA in downtown Montreal that serves as a shelter for refugee claimants. She later took the initiative of putting together welcome packets and delivered them to refugees when they moved out of the shelter.

Anne emailed Marc and Kim Wyatt, Cooperative Baptist Fellowship workers in Ottawa to tell them about Christine. She also emailed Christine to say, "You need to meet the Wyatts." The Wyatts soon met with Christine in a small coffee shop in Montreal and immediately gave her their full support. They sealed their first meeting with a time of enthusiastic prayer. The Wyatts also knew of Christopher Lu's passion for a Matthew House and conspired to get Christopher and Christine together. The opportunity came in November, 2009, at the MissionsFest ("Missions Globales") meeting in Montreal. Marc, Kim, Christopher and Christine sat down over coffee to talk about their vision and calling for Montreal. Christopher laid out the plan he had been thinking about for several years and talked about the portion of his budget that he had been setting aside in preparation for this project. What was lacking was a person to connect with the refugees. Christine shared her call to be that kind of person. It was done. Two callings merged into one.

Christopher's business plan called for starting small, renting an apartment rather than purchasing a house like other places. He said, "I will pay for the apartment and be the one to introduce it to the churches in the area." Marc and Kim said, "We will wrap around that and support you in whatever way we can." They called a meeting of churches to share their dream. They elected a Board of directors and began the process of getting non-profit status. Westmount Baptist Church agreed to take the ministry under their umbrella until that status was acquired. CBOQ leaders came alongside the project with grant money to help cover some of the costs. The well-thought-out plan was falling in place . . . or was it?

THE LANDSCAPE CHANGES

The Matthew House apartment opened on March 1, 2010, just four months after the initial meeting between Christopher and Christine. It was located a few blocks from Christine's home where she would have quick access in the evenings after her regular social work job each day. But the excitement of the new refugee residence quickly faded. The apartment remained empty for an entire month. Where were the refugees?

The opening of Matthew House Montreal coincided with increased restrictions that were placed on immigration by the Canadian and Quebec governments. The numbers of refugees coming into Montreal was greatly reduced. Christine said, "It's not that they can't come in, many just don't know how." For a while Quebec was receiving refugee claimants from Mexico. Now they were required to have visas to enter, which made it impossible to get to Canada to make a claim. Also, refugees transitioning through a third country like the United States were no longer allowed to make a claim in Canada. Refugee claimants coming via the Canada/United States border were no longer admitted to the country if they didn't have a relative already in the country.

In the past, PRAIDA (Programme régional d'accueil et d'intégration des demandeurs d'asile), the government program responsible for refugee claimants in Montreal, funded one main refugee shelter at the YWCA in downtown Montreal as well as a number of smaller shelters that catered to unaccompanied minors and more vulnerable refugee claimants. As a result of the new immigration restrictions, PRAIDA eventually stopped funding all but one of the smaller shelters. Christine said, "At first I was discouraged thinking everything is shutting down. But now I see that God was using us because we are not government funded. I have a sense that God is going to use Matthew House as a place that remains a family environment where vulnerable people can come." In addition, the Matthew House Board made a conscious decision to enlarge their plan and serve newcomers who needed a place to live whether or not they were technically refugee claimants.

Christine found an agency working with Haitian earthquake victims who were allowed into the country. The Quebec government permitted Haitian people who had Canadian children to accompany their children into the province. These adults had no status at all, not even refugee status. That meant that access to welfare or other social services was a complicated process. Two of these families moved into Matthew House Montreal. Because of their special status, the Board allowed them to live in the apartment longer than the original plan called for despite the fact that they initially had no income to help pay the ongoing costs. Christine and others advocated tirelessly for these two families who eventually were able to make refugee claims and were subsequently able to get their own places to live.

WHAT THE FUTURE HOLDS

Matthew House Montreal's first year was a learning experience for everyone involved. A step at a time, they've moved from a joint vision to a house full of refugees who needed welcome. At this point, they have found a new location near the city centre. The immediate task at hand is to fix up the place to make it a warm, hospitable environment for the new residents. Christine pointed out that other challenges remain—establishing a broader base of volunteers as well as increasing their partnerships with churches and service agencies that help refugees. She knows that it will all come in God's time. Each day is a new challenge. "It's fun to follow God," Christine said. "It really feels like that. We kind of half know the plan, but we don't know it all. We're excited to see how it's going to turn out."

I Am Alone.

Christopher Lu was born into a middle class Christian family in Saigon Vietnam during the Vietnam War. He had a loving family and a good private education that took him through the twelfth grade. When United States forces pulled out of South Vietnam in 1974 his life crumbled. The new Communist regime closed down all the banks and nationalized all the stores, schools and universities.

Like every other family, the government issued a booklet of coupons used to purchase small portions of food to Christopher's family. They stood in long lines to get enough food to barely stay alive. "My family survived by eating rice mixed with salt and sesame seeds," he said. In addition, they ate watermelon rinds as a substitute for vegetables. Christopher sold instant noodles and boxes of matches on the street to earn what little cash he could.

In 1976, Christopher escaped on a boat packed with 100 refugees bound for Indonesia. There he stayed in a refugee camp for over a year where he got only rice and cabbage to eat. Despite tons of aid sent by United Nations relief efforts, little made its way to the refugees. Finally, in 1978, Christopher was accepted into Canada. He believed all his worries were over.

Instead of hope, he found more heartache. He had no friends or relatives to rely on in Canada, no one to turn to for guidance and help. Although he had a High School education, he couldn't find work. The winter was colder than he ever imagined possible. "I cried at night and prayed to God," he said. "I want to go home. At least in Vietnam I still had friends and relatives who could help me, but here I am alone."

One day a neighbor from the apartment where he lived with other refugees approached him about a job. He said he was the manager of a plant and would give Christopher a job in exchange for sexual relations. Christopher refused. Eventually, he landed a minimum wage job as a clerk. For several years he worked and went to night school until he received his Masters Degree in Business Administration.

Today, Christopher is a successful businessman who has a heart for refugees. In 2002 he met Anne Woolger and began to dream and pray about a Matthew House in Montreal. In 2009, he partnered with Christine Walsh to make it happen. It was Christopher's business plan and initial funding that got it off the ground so quickly. Matthew House Montreal is barely a year old, but Christopher is already thinking about his next big project. He wants to open an orphanage in Southeast Asia for abandoned children.

Christopher Lu

The Earthquake Changed My Life

Dorice and her 11-year-old daughter, Clara, have lived in the Montreal Matthew House for about a year. They are from Haiti. During our interview, Dorice sat next to an open window, her face silhouetted in the bright sunlight. As I asked her questions, she shyly answered, using Christine as her interpreter. Christine helped to engage her and she began to talk more. Later, her daughter sat in the same chair while I asked her questions. She was more confident and articulate with her answers, eager to tell the details of the story.

On Tuesday, January 12, 2010 a 7.0 magnitude earthquake struck Haiti, 16 miles from Port —au-Prince, the capital city. That day Clara was sitting on the balcony of her home. She heard a loud sound she could not identify. Then other sounds came that she thought were people arguing (probably shouts from other parts of the neighborhood). Suddenly the earth and the balcony began to shake. She fell, but she doesn't know if she fell down because of the shaking or because of her fright. The house across the street collapsed. She remembered seeing a woman not far away with her hand on a wall and the other hand on an iron railing. The wall simply disappeared leaving the woman standing there clinging to the rail. Dorice came from inside their home and fell on top of Clara to protect her. She and her mother cried, "Jesus help us." Clara said, "The earthquake changed my life completely,"

When the shaking ceased Dorice and Clara tried to go through the door to get off the balcony, but the door wouldn't open. They were both crying. They prayed for Jesus' help and the door opened. They were able to get out of their home before it collapsed. Clara explained that, as they were leaving, they had to cross over a large crevice in the ground to get to the street.

Clara had a terrible headache and discovered that her foot had been injured. Her mother bandaged the wound as best as she could. The streets were full of people running in every direction. Many were bleeding. Clara was concerned about finding another woman who was like a second mother to her. In the midst of the chaos, they finally found her alive and they were greatly relieved.

That night the two slept on the street. Clara had difficulty sleeping because her head was hurting so badly. At one point during the night she vomited. Eventually she slept but it was very uncomfortable. They ended up sleeping on the streets for a few days. While there, another small quake hit and the earth shook again. As Clara told their story in great detail, I could picture the devastation, fear and pain. I noticed Dorice staring out the window, her eyes tearing up in the remembering.

Because Clara's father was a Canadian, she and her mother qualified to relocate to Canada and escape the dangers in Haiti. When they came to Canada they stayed with members of her husband's family for a few days. That family had their own chaos and seemed to resent Dorice and Clara's presence. They felt unwanted and terribly stressed. In a short period of time they experienced the trauma of a major earthquake and the aftermath of its chaos. They were uprooted and transported to a new country away from their family and friends. Then, they shared a home where they were not welcome.

Finally, an agency that works with Haitians referred them to Matthew House. Dorice said that Matthew House is their mother. It has provided them a safe place to find healing and help. When Dorice and Clara came to Matthew House all their chaos disappeared. It was replaced with love, peace and hope. Dorice said she felt like Jesus was with her, that Jesus had somehow chosen her and that he would continue to be with her and Clara.

Matthew House has provided them support and helped Dorice negotiate the appropriate systems to apply for refugee status. She can't go home because of all the violence that remains there. The trauma has visibly worn on Dorice. She said she still has her ups and downs—her dark moods and bad days, but the people of Matthew House accept her for who she is, without judging her.

Although life was hard before the earthquake, Clara did have friends and loved ones around her that she misses now. Clara is adjusting more quickly than her mother. She has friends in Canada. She loves school and is a thriving "A" student. The love she has received at Matthew House provided her with the support she needed to heal from the trauma she experienced. Although Dorice has not yet been able to find work, mother and daughter are grateful for what God has done in their lives and they feel hopeful about their future.

CHAPTER 6

MATTHEW HOUSE OTTAWA

Marc Wyatt and Glenn Hawley

At Eglise Evangelique Baptiste d'Ottawa (EGEBO) about 600 people walk through its doors every Sunday. The Sunday morning I visited, the small sanctuary overflowed with worshipers. I stood with others, unable to move, in a packed small foyer, waiting for the pastor's prayer to end so ushers could try to find more seats for the throng waiting to get in. Although I couldn't understand the French language, I could understand the presence of God's Spirit among those who raised their voices in song and prayed deep, heart-felt prayers.

EGEBO, a church of the L'Union d'Églises Baptistes Françaises au Canada (Union of French Baptists of Canada), has not always been this crowded. During 2006-2007 the United States cracked down on undocumented residents, many of whom had lived in the United States for many years. They had jobs and families and considered the U.S. their home. But their undocumented status left them vulnerable to U.S. government exportation. In addition, they were unable to apply for refugee status due to new laws that had been imposed, which denied anyone the right to apply if they had lived in the United States for more than one year. Close to 50,000 people left the U.S. for Canada. Many of these were French-speaking Haitians who made their way to Ottawa, Ontario where they had connections with other Haitian refugees. Almost overnight the church exploded with new members, most of whom had basic unmet needs.

Through the grace of God, EGEBO had a plan in place. In February, 2005, Pastor Frankie Narcisse recognized that church member Benito Bastien had a heart for social ministry and asked him to write a proposal to organize the church's community life. The church approved Benito's proposal, but there was no money to implement it. Sometimes we seem to reach dead ends in ministry. We see something we believe needs to be done, something we believe God desires of us. We put time and energy into it, only to have it come to nothing—or so it seems. Rather than let the project die, the church decided to pray and let God work it out in God's time.

EGEBO couldn't have known that within a very short time God would send more people than they could possibly serve. God knew before they did and prepared his servants for a caring ministry. God sees what we can't see. He knows the future. He knows what the needs of humanity will be tomorrow and next year. He uses churches that are willing to listen, prepare and wait for God to perform wondrous miracles in their places of worship.

A NETWORK OF MINISTRIES

God was at work on another front as well. After conversations with Canadian Baptist Ministries (CBM) and the discovery of the need for workers among French-speaking Canadians and refugees, Marc and Kim Wyatt moved from Toronto to Ottawa just as the refugees were arriving. When Pastor Frankie Narcisse heard that Marc and Kim had come, he introduced himself and pulled them into the ministry that the church was trying to provide for the huge influx of Haitians. In one meeting, Frankie said, "Marc, we need a Matthew House right now, tonight." At that moment, below them in the church's fellowship hall Benito Bastien was visiting with 87 refugees who were describing their needs—they required help with getting lawyers, filling out immigration papers, getting furniture when they moved out of crowded shelters, medical care, backpacks for school and much more.

Although a Matthew House was not possible at that moment, they decided that night to put out a call to CBOQ churches, other Great Commission Christians, social and governmental organizations and area businesses to rally around the needs of the people coming to Evangelique Baptiste for help. They called the new group "Réseau Mathieu 25:35," the Matthew 25:35 Network. They understood that, although the housing component of Matthew House ministries was not an option at that time, they could still perform many other loving, caring ministries that refugees needed. They moved forward with the vision of "encouraging a Christ-like welcome by being the presence of Christ among the refugee community of the Capital Region."

Marc started going to garage sales and estate sales where he casually asked, "What are you going to do with the stuff that doesn't sell?" Then he offered to pick up what was left over. He started getting many donations which he stacked under his carport and on his driveway. He enlisted volunteers to pick up and haul furniture. Pastor Benito brought families by to get furniture for their empty apartments. Over the next few years, this small furniture ministry became a network of over 30 agencies, organizations and businesses. It is now located in a donated warehouse and has served over 6000 people.

THE COST OF MINISTRY

Throughout this time, Benito Bastien made numerous personal connections with the refugees coming to his church for help. They started calling him day and night, at home and at work, to share their needs. His own wife and five children saw less and less of him. His boss at the social service agency where he worked became irritated at the number of calls he received every day. Finally, his boss confronted him. "Are you a pastor or do you work here as a social worker?" For Benito, it wasn't an either/or issue. "I think the church has two missions," he says, "a social mission and a spiritual mission."

Regardless, the calls had to stop. Soon after, when Benito took a day off, his voice mailbox filled up with 46 messages. When his boss discovered it, he fired Benito. His ministry to the arriving refugees cost him his job. Now the question was not how he was going to care for the refugee needs, but how he was going to care for his own family. Although EGEBO didn't have the funds and didn't know where they would come from, they hired Benito as their Associate Pastor. God supplied the necessary funds, which allowed Benito to give full attention to refugee newcomers and the administration of the welcoming ministry plan he had formulated.

Benito told of this journey with a smile on his face and laughter in his eyes because he has no doubt that God walks with him in all he does. Even in the difficulties of life, we can be assured that God is at work leading us and preparing us for the next step or the next phase of our lives. The joy Benito receives through his ministry is contagious. He shared stories where his ministry made real differences—things like locating medical supplies and arranging for a much needed blood transfusion that saved lives. So is the loss of a job because of ministry a bad thing? For Benito, it opened up many more doors for ministry. He would say, "Praise God."

A MATTHEW HOUSE

Despite the successes of the Matthew 25:35 Network and the ministries of Eglise Evangelique Baptiste, Ottawa still didn't have a Matthew House. And having a house was still part of their dream. Al Turcott, husband of the pastor of Bethany Baptist Church, helped in the furniture ministry when he was between jobs. The church owned a 112-year-old vacant farmhouse next door to their building. After Al saw the needs of the refugees he said to his church, "Why don't we make this a Matthew House?" They formed a committee that conducted deliberations and did research and feasibility studies. The negotiations to make the farm house into a Matthew House began in February 2009.

Simultaneously, an eight member Matthew House Board was formed to work on all the necessary details—officially establishing Matthew House Ottawa. The Board applied for registered charitable status and worked out the lease agreement with Bethany Baptist. The Board is chaired by Steven Kuhn, a member of the Meeting House Church. Before coming to Ottawa, Steven and his wife Laura were missionaries to Mozambique. He said that one of the greatest things they learned as missionaries was that "the easiest and most lasting way to make a difference in the world is to do so at home, within one's own culture. We can have a huge impact on our world by serving the powerless and poor within our own community."

In June 2010, Bethany Baptist gave the Matthew House Board access to the home. Marc Wyatt says of that time that "It's not just that a bunch of people said, 'Let's go get a house.' It's that God was at work in a bunch of people's lives, reaching out to people that were refugees. At some juncture in that call, they decided as part of what they did already, they could also do the house."

Under the supervisory leadership of Glenn Hawley from McPhail Baptist Church, the renovations began. Glenn said, "I have never ever worked on a project where I didn't know what the skill level was going to be. I didn't know if I was going to have the material. I didn't know if I had to wait to see if I could get it for free. I didn't know what the budget was." It was truly an act of faith and help came from every corner. The Manotick United Church stepped up and donated $5000 to help launch the renovation. In addition, volunteers came from churches, Habitat for Humanity supplied some experienced carpenters and opened their "ReStore" for free access to materials. Home Depot provided gift cards. Local plumbing and electric firms provided free labour. A local company donated and installed kitchen and bathroom cabinets for free. A flooring company donated the flooring and two local architects donated their architectural services.

The volunteers put in a completely new kitchen, a new kitchen/dining room floor, and a laundry room. They converted two half baths into two full baths and another half bath and turned four bedrooms into five. Finally, they installed a new larger gas water heater and ran hundreds of feet of new wiring. In the end, they completed a $50,000 renovation project for only $11,000.

In the beginning, when the Board was discussing how to go about supervising the house, they felt the need for house parents, individuals willing to live in the house to care for the day to day needs of the residents. Board member, Keith Dow volunteered to move his family into the house. Keith and Darcie, his wife, would provide consistency and a family feel to the home.

In addition to the Dows, volunteers took turns acting as interim director one day a week during the first months. Kim Wyatt remembers thinking they needed one steady, passionate person to give leadership in the house. There wasn't enough consistency. Details were falling through the cracks. Kim thought that person was Jan Mills. She said, "My prayer was, 'Lord, Jan is the obvious person in my mind. Is there any way that she would be able to give more time?" Not long after, Jan told Kim in confidence, "I think I might be able to give more time in the New Year." Starting January 1, 2011 she gave three days a week to Matthew House. Immediately, the rhythm of the house changed to consistency and order. Just recently, the Board hired Jan as Matthew House Ottawa's first Executive Director.

A DIFFERENT PATH

Every Matthew House has its own path. For Ottawa, that path began with a church that had a heart for Haitian refugees and a plan for ministry, but no resources. Rather than starting with a house, they chose to start with ministries to meet the ongoing needs. They worked tirelessly and faithfully, even when the cost was great. They gathered other caring people around them and chose to work together. The house was always a matter of prayer, but God provided the house when the time was right.

While Marc Wyatt was giving my wife and me a tour of the new 3200 square foot Furniture Bank warehouse, he talked about the struggle to get where they are. God didn't give them everything right away. He said, "It is as if God was testing us to see if we would faithfully stay with it. When we did, he blessed us beyond measure." It reminded me of Jesus' parable in Matthew 25 in which the Master gives his servants each a few talents before leaving on a trip. When he returns he says to those who have faithfully used the talents, "Well done, good and faithful servant! You have been faithful with a few things; I will put you in charge of many things. Come and share your master's happiness!" What a joy to know that when we faithfully serve, our Master invites us to join in his happiness.

Marc puts it a different way, "God knew how to line us all up. Then we took the little loaves and fishes we had, because we were just the little boy at the big meeting. We had nothing. We took it and we blessed it and we said, 'Lord use this.' He took those little things and he multiplied them a thousand times."

Matthew House also operates a
3,200 square foot Furniture Bank
in Ottawa.

Destined for Ministry

Benito Bastien was born in a small village in Haiti. Although his mother came from poor country roots, his father came from a wealthy Anglican family. Due to his mother's roots in poverty she was never well accepted into his father's side of the family. As a result, Benito can remember feeling the rejection. "I felt like this small family was a refugee family within a larger family."

Despite his difficult start, Benito grew up a man of faith and entered the seminary to become an Anglican priest. Along the journey, he became a financial manager of a big technology assembly factory in Haiti, supervising 12-15 accountants. One of his regular jobs included picking up large amounts of payroll cash from the bank to distribute to employees. One day the bank owner asked him to go to the bank to take care of other business that involved opening a new account. When he left the bank, kidnappers who thought he was carrying cash assaulted him.

At the time, Benito's wife was pregnant with their fourth child. The owner of the bank told him to take two months paid vacation to go somewhere to recuperate. He took his family to Canada. While there, he continued to hear stories of kidnappings and assaults, so he and his family decided to stay in Canada. Since their money was quickly running out, they moved to a motel for homeless people where they stayed for 45 days. Then Benito set about learning the process refugees must go through in order to immigrate.

Because of the difficulties he and his family suffered, he has a heart for refugees, especially those coming out of Haiti. God placed him at Eglise Evangelique Baptiste d'Ottawa at the right moment in time to help Pastor Frankie Narcisse develop a ministry plan that God used to help the flood of refugees that came into Canada in 2006-2007. Today, Benito serves as co-pastor of a new church plant in a multicultural neighbourhood.

GRATITUDE LIVED OUT

David came to the United States from Zimbabwe in 1996 to get an education. While in school the political strife back home escalated. Because of papers he wrote, lectures he gave and positions that he took in conversations with ex-militia from Zimbabwe, he felt it was unsafe to return to his country. "Mugabe has always had a fear of teachers that they are able to influence minds," he said. "I felt it was a wise thing for me not to go back."

When his education visa ran out, David had to choose whether to return to Zimbabwe or seek refuge in Canada. He made the long road trip from Houston, TX to Buffalo, New York and crossed the border into Ft. Erie. A helpful immigration officer pointed him to Matthew House. "When I got to Matthew House," he said, "I was really surprised to find this well-kept house. Everything was laid out—food and comfortable accommodation. Jim and Shirley McNair welcomed everyone. They didn't pry into people's business too much, but the Christian element was strong. It didn't matter what denomination, what religion, or what sect you came from. You were welcomed at Matthew House."

During his month at Matthew House, David got all the help he needed from Jim and Shirley. They arranged for his medical check-ups, appointments with legal aid and lawyers and paperwork to complete in order to gain his refugee status. David's gratitude for their love and help continued after he moved out of Matthew House. He returned to visit Jim and Shirley often and volunteered some of his time. Eventually, he returned as their night manager.

David now is in Ottawa where he serves the Matthew House there.

He brings expertise and compassion to this new ministry. He believes his own experience helps him understand the difficulties refugees go through so that he can effectively relate to those coming to Matthew House. He is clear when he speaks about his experience that he is "still learning from others who come to Matthew House because people's circumstances are so different. Working in such an establishment, trying to understand the cultural differences, trying to accommodate everybody and their needs can be quite a challenge. I don't think anyone can ever get to a stage where they are totally are comfortable."

David

David is willing to try. He no longer wants to teach, which was his first ambition. Today he's more interested in social work and in helping people out. The Matthew House experience changed the course of his life.

An Emotional Meeting

Story telling is an important part of ministry for God's people because it's in the telling that we remember the goodness of God. These were some of my thoughts as I sat at Marc and Kim Wyatt's dining room table listening as they swapped tales with Glenn and Doris Hawley. A contest seemed to be going on between Marc and Glenn to see who could remember the most details. I simply listened as they fed off each other while describing picking up furniture together for the furniture bank and detailing the renovation of Matthew House Ottawa which Marc talked Glenn into supervising.

They were wonderful God-stories, stories of faithful servants using their gifts to make a difference, stories of God's abundance of gifts that were necessary to make the renovation a success. They spoke of individuals whose lives were touched through their volunteer work at the house. They spoke of struggles, setbacks and mutual encouragement along the way. On several occasions we all burst into laughter at their comical effort to outdo each other.

About half way through the conversation, Hiwot, a shy Ethiopian woman joined us. She was introduced to Glenn as the first refugee to live in Matthew House Ottawa. Glenn spent three months working with wood, electrical wiring, plumbing, flooring and cabinets while supervising the Matthew House renovation project, but he had not yet met this woman who benefitted from all his labor. It was hard to tell what Glenn was thinking. He was quiet now, the stories on hold as we all contemplated the force of the meeting.

Hiwot had been on the refugee highway for 13 years before finally landing in Ottawa. She lived with Marc and Kim for a week before Matthew House officially opened and was, according to them, the model resident.

Although Hiwot speaks several languages, her English was hesitant, "It's hard for me to express the love," she said. "I'm thankful to Jesus. I'm excited and very happy. I'm very lucky. It was a good time for me in Matthew House. It was not just a shelter for refugees. It was freedom and love." Then she switched to her native Amharic language where she felt she could express herself more fully. Although no one around the table could understand her words, we had no doubt the gratitude was genuine and deep as tears welled up in her eyes.

Marc then turned his attention to Glenn. "The history books are going to say it was men like you from churches like yours that heard the call and stepped up and made a place for people that God was bringing from far away, like Hiwot, to come and live in this city."

At the end of the evening, Hiwot prayed a prayer of thanksgiving in her native language. When we heard Amen, Marc pointed out that it was 2000 years ago that a man believed in Jesus. He returned to his land and shared the Gospel with the Queen of Ethiopia. Tonight a Christian from Ethiopia blessed our time together. *Joey Clifton*

Hiwot

CHAPTER 7

CONTINUING THE MOVEMENT
WHERE YOU LIVE

Marc and Kim Wyatt

Marc and Kim Wyatt felt God's call to missions. Faithfully they pursued the correct theological education, made the appropriate applications and received an appointment from the Cooperative Baptist Fellowship to be missionaries to Thailand. They left their "southern" middle class roots and traveled half way around the world where they spent a year in torturous language school to prepare for their immersion into a very different culture from the place where they grew up.

They did all this because that's what they believed missionaries do. Missionaries go. Everyone else stays home and prays for them or gives money to support them. Most of us grew up with this missional model. It's a model that has firm Biblical roots. Didn't Jesus tell us in Matthew 28:19: "Therefore go and make disciples of all nations"? Didn't the first century church send out Paul to travel across Asia Minor spreading the Good News while they stayed home and prayed?

When Marc and Kim were abruptly brought home from Thailand by CBF in 1998 before even having a chance to begin their ministry there, they were confused. When they were appointed to Toronto to work with Anne Woolger at Matthew House Toronto, they were even more confused. Toronto? Really? It is a foreign country for one raised in the United States. But Canada is not a third world country? Canada has more than 19,000 Christian churches from coast to coast to coast. Kim says, "I never would have left Virginia where we lived before we were appointed to come to Canada. That was not what I thought going on mission and being a missionary meant."

A New Way of Thinking

Once in Toronto, they found people from all over the world sitting together around a dinner table or sharing intimate moments in the living room of Matthew House. These people, many of whom had no previous opportunity to hear about God's love, had begun to see it lived out in observable and practical ways. The house residents often asked Marc and Kim, "Why do you do this? What's in it for you?" Marc says, "That's the question every missionary wants to hear. That opens the door." They found themselves doing exactly what they had been trained to do—sharing God's love in easily understandable ways to people who were listening. They started looking at everyone who came through the Matthew House doors as sent there by God.

Their understanding of missions took on a dramatic change. "From that time forward our vision of missions shifted from going to a particular geographical area to seeing the people that were coming from all over," said Marc. "From that point forward it wasn't about where you go. It is God calling his people to all the peoples of the world all of the time, wherever we happen to be and wherever they happen to be."

This is a radical truth that Anne Woolger grasped early in her ministry. One of her initial career possibilities was to be a missionary, which meant going overseas somewhere. She even took a year to test out the possibilities in Japan. God had different ideas for her. God put her to work in a homeless shelter in downtown Toronto where she encountered refugee claimants from all over the world. "I realized the world was arriving on our doorstep," she said.

Missions is here as well as there. It's welcoming the stranger in Jesus' name, reaching out to those who need food, shelter, clothing and the love of God. Kim Wyatt points out that "You're crossing cultures all the time; you're just not thinking about it in a missional way." Refugees are on the move all across the globe looking for a safe place to live. They are fleeing persecution, death, starvation and torture. They come from Muslim, Buddhist, Hindu, Animist and Christian cultures. Many are finding a home at the end of the Refugee Highway in Canada. Fifty-four percent of Toronto residents were not born in Canada. But refugees are in all of our Canadian cities.

The question begging to be asked is "What are Christians doing to welcome and minister to these people?" First Baptist Church in Ft. Erie and Grace Baptist in Windsor made a conscious decision to meet the needs of those coming to their cities. Together they have touched the lives of almost 2000 refugees. Their churches have been transformed into houses of prayer for all nations. Other churches, like Bethany Baptist and McPhail Baptist in Ottawa and Westmount Baptist in Montreal are new at this, but they are catching the vision and committing resources to minister to those who live at their doorstep.

EXPANDING THE MATTHEW HOUSE MOVEMENT

When I asked Anne Woolger what her vision for the Matthew House future was, she said, "I sometimes call us a 'Centre of Hope at the end of the Refugee Highway.' I see us as a welcoming place, but also as a model of ministry to inspire others because I would love to see more refugees welcomed in Jesus' name." Indeed, Anne's model has inspired many people to welcome refugees in Jesus name. This book describes Anne's work in Toronto and in four other Matthew Houses that the CBOQ helped sponsor in one way or another. There are others places across Canada under different names that were inspired by the Matthew House Toronto model, but Anne doesn't keep count, as if they are somehow her children. She is clear that the Matthew House Movement is God's story—she only plays a part.

Although the Matthew Houses are built from a common inspiration and share experiences with one another, each is unique. Each operates in its own way, meeting the specific needs of a particular situation. Matthew House is not a program you can initiate. There is no cookie cutter plan that works in every situation. A Matthew House is the kingdom of God at work in your community. It is the active living of Matthew 25 by Christians who care deeply about hearing the urging of God. Because listening to God's call is what is required, not every situation may need a house. Ottawa churches banded together for several years to minister to refugee claimants before a house came together. What God desires from each of us is what he told Anne Woolger in some of her darkest moments: "House or no house, what I really want is for you to know me and to walk with me. . . ."

A MATTHEW HOUSE IN YOUR TOWN

Although each Matthew House is different, the experiences of the houses described in this book provide us with some lessons for those who feel the call of God to begin a refugee ministry. At first glance, it might not appear that way. Consider the differences. Some took years to realize. Others were opened in a matter of a few months. Some of the ministries own the houses; others rent. One is not a house at all, but an apartment. Each has its own array of staff members who have responsibilities that dramatically differ from one place to the next. Each has different funding sources and sustainability plans. The list can go on, but this is not particularly helpful for those who want to begin their own Matthew House ministry, except to assure you that there is no one right way to do this.

But there are key lessons we can pull together, perhaps we should call them themes or checkpoints along the way that create a roadmap for developing a Matthew House in your town.

1 **Respond to God's Spirit.** God's call is universal and particular. That is, there are some things all of us as Christians are called to do; there are some things God calls specific individuals to do. All of us are called to love God with all our heart and love our neighbour as ourselves. We are called to share the Gospel message with those who have not heard. We are called, in Matthew 25, to feed the hungry, give drink to the thirsty, welcome the stranger,

clothe the naked, tend the sick and visit prisoners. In other words, we are all called to care for those in need just as Christ did. Caring for the refugees who live around you falls within this universal calling. When we do it to those whose lives are broken and in despair, we do it unto Christ.

Each of us also has particular skills and gifts to offer to a Matthew House ministry. Matthew House ministries need accountants, food preparers, renovators, administrators, drivers, listeners, financial givers, prayers, promoters, fund raisers, furniture movers, encouragers and hosts. The list is endless. We mustn't think that, just because we can't be a house director, we can't do anything. When Anne Woolger first felt the urge of the Holy Spirit to respond to refugee claimants, she found a place that worked with refugees and volunteered the next day.

2   **Become a champion.** I'm reminded of what Joanne King called her Moses Experience. She gave God all her excuses, one of which was that she didn't know anything about refugees. By reading this book, you know more about refugees than she did when she committed herself to the Matthew House ministry in Windsor. She was a retired teacher who deserved a little rest. She wasn't looking for another career. In the end, she put aside her excuses and followed the leadership of God. Without Joanne the idea for a Matthew House in Windsor might have never moved beyond the initial discussions.

A successful Matthew House ministry requires champions, people to boldly follow the leadership of God. They are retired teachers, business people, social workers, housewives, retired engineers—people who listened to God and responded faithfully. Champions are not just those who lead the ministry. Often, they are behind the scenes renovating buildings, fixing meals, serving on Boards, providing transportation, hauling furniture, or holding the hand of a distraught refugee.

Champions are people who don't give up. They continue to believe in the power and movement of God even when things aren't going as planned. In the darkest, most discouraging days, they don't lose faith. They persevere with the deep belief that God is in control of every situation and will provide when the time is right. I think of Anne Woolger's darkest days when it looked like her vision of a Matthew House would never materialize. At that point she gave it all to God. "House or no house, I simply want to walk with God." I think of Benito Bastien who lost his job caring for the Haitian refugees flooding into Ottawa yet persisted in the ministry. I remember Joanne King telling me of the flood that destroyed their newly renovated house that forced them to start all over.

Champions persist because they believe in the faithfulness of God. They remember the marvellous way God has worked in the past and know that he is the same yesterday, today and forever. God will continue to provide. This knowledge allows them to step out in faith even when they don't know where next month's rent money is coming from or how they are going to feed their residents. Each time they step out in faith, God provides. His provision inspires people like Anne Woolger to tell God-story after God-story until there is no doubt in our mind that truly the whole Matthew House movement is God's Story.

3 **Discover specific needs.** When Marc and Kim Wyatt first met Benito Bastien he was in the basement of their church listening to 87 Haitian refugees tell him their needs. "We need lawyers, someone to help us with immigration paperwork, housing, transportation, food, furniture, and school supplies," they said. He wrote down all their needs and responded to them that night, "I can't promise anything, but we are praying that God will send us help to meet your needs." The 87 in the room turned into 100, 200, then 300 as the refugees continued to come and their needs continued to mount.

Anne Woolger's original vision grew out of needs she was seeing in the shelter where she worked. She saw that sponsored refugees were taken care of, but refugee claimants had no place to go, no one to help them and no access to furniture. She saw the need and dreamed of a way to meet it.

First Baptist Church Ft. Erie discovered that 8000 refugees a year were coming across the border into their city and there was only one small shelter with 8 beds. They discovered that refugee claimants were not always treated with dignity at the border and resolved to work on a solution.

Every situation, every city or town, is different. One of the first steps of a Matthew House ministry is to discover those needs. Talk to agencies that work with refugees. Educate yourself about the current services being provided and the gaps in services that need to be filled. Contact your denomination's affiliate organizations to see if there are other churches in your area that are working with refugees to see how you might partner or add to that ministry. Go to places and parts of town where refugees might live. Strike up conversations and get to know some of them. Moving from a statistical study of numbers and group needs to a personal level of individual relationships helps us better grasp the life experience of refugees.

4   **Do what it takes to meet the needs.** A Matthew House was not an option for Ottawa at first, but that didn't stop Marc Wyatt from gathering furniture at garage and estate sales. It didn't keep Benito Bastien from taking calls and assisting the needs of those he could. Even with a house, the needs of refugees go far beyond the immediate housing necessity. Jim Mc-Nair spends hours every week transporting refugee claimants to doctor appointments, immigration appointments, or to the store. He transports furniture and performs handyman work. Anne Woolger volunteered her time to meet whatever needs there were. Even before they had a Matthew House in Montreal, Christine Walsh put together welcome bags to give to refugees.

Refugee needs are abundant. Fulfilling those needs doesn't always require highly organized or structured activities. Helping others with their needs does require compassion and the willingness to move beyond our comfort zone to enter into another person's life. Successful Matthew House ministries always start with individuals who not only take the time to discover the needs of refugees, but commit themselves to finding solutions for those needs, regardless of the cost. They simply refuse to give up.

5   **Gather Partners.** Although much can be done by one person, when Christians work together in one accord, wondrous miracles take place. None of the Matthew Houses described in this book is the work of one individual. Canadian Christians together joined God in work that needed to be done. Anne Woolger had a wonderful vision, but she needed the help of the CBOQ and people like Larry Matthews. The House in Windsor started with like-minded, caring individuals from several churches. In Montreal, God placed the vision in the hearts of two individuals who didn't know each other. It took the work of a third party to bring them together. In Ottawa, the work started with a church associated with the Union of French Speaking Baptist Churches before CBOQ churches caught the vision and joined in. When they began their Matthew 25:35 Network they had Mennonites, Pentecostals, and local business people. Wow, one might think the Kingdom of God had arrived. Indeed, it has!

Each Matthew House put together a steering committee that later became their Board. They were individuals who shared the dream, spent a great deal of time in prayer and set out a shared plan that they could work on together. Most started with a simple meeting to share the idea. They invited Anne Woolger to speak or they heard from local refugees. Yes, someone had to cast the vision, share the dream and speak God's call to his people, but the work is always done by the church, the body of Christ.

After you spend time in prayer and in listening to the strangers in your midst, make a list of potential partners. Your list might include churches in your association, outside your denomination, regional or national church leadership, local agencies and Baptist women organizations. Allow your mind to be open to the fact that God can work through all his people regardless of language or affiliation.

6 **Organize and Make a Plan.** For a Matthew House ministry to be successful it requires carefully thought out plans with the understanding that God may change those plans along the way. Here are some of the many issues that need to be addressed:

- How do we get non-profit status and what organization would fulfill that role for us until our status is secured?
- What is our budget?
- How are we going to fund the ministry?
- Should we purchase a house or rent one?
- Where should the house be located?
- What specific ministries are we going to attempt to do? Will we simply do housing or will we provide help with immigration, furniture, transportation and other needs?
- What staff do we need?
- Who will supervise the house when paid staff is not present?
- How will we recruit volunteers?

This list is just a start. Your planning group will think of many more issues related to your specific situation. A great way to make sure your list of questions is complete is to talk to Board members of the Matthew Houses already in operation. They can point you to the major concerns and offer you suggestions on how they might be handled. Lean on each other. Seek out others who have gone before you.

7 **Pray and Act.** I hope you've already figured out that you can do none of this without spending time together in prayer seeking God's direction and activity. You want to join God, not tell God how you want to do it. Prayer is at the core of every powerful Christian movement. Anne Woolger spent many hours in prayer over her dream trying to figure out God's calling and direction. Christine Walsh prayed for people to come along side her and God provided Christopher Lu. Bethany Baptist in Ottawa had two prayer warriors named Maria and Lolita. The prayers of these two Pilipino sisters were instrumental in bringing Bethany Baptist to offer their old vacant farmhouse to be renovated into a Matthew House.

Although praying will never cease and all the details will never be in place, at some point you must take a step of faith and act. Remember the words of James in the New Testament:

What good is it, my brothers and sisters, if people claim to have faith but have no deeds? Can such faith save them? Suppose a brother or sister is without clothes and daily food. If one of you says to them, "Go in peace; keep warm and well fed," but does nothing about their physical needs, what good is it? In the same way, faith by itself, if it is not accompanied by action, is dead. (James 2:14-17)

Begin the ministry and trust God with the results. Some communities may be deliberate and work through everything with painstaking detail. That's fine, as long as planning doesn't become an end in itself. Other communities may move more quickly like Christine Walsh and Christopher Lu did in Montreal. Remember Christine's words: "It's fun to follow God. We kind of half know the plan, but we don't know it all. We're excited to see how it's going to turn out." Following God in faith truly is an adventure, and one you can be involved in by responding to the Spirit's call in your life.

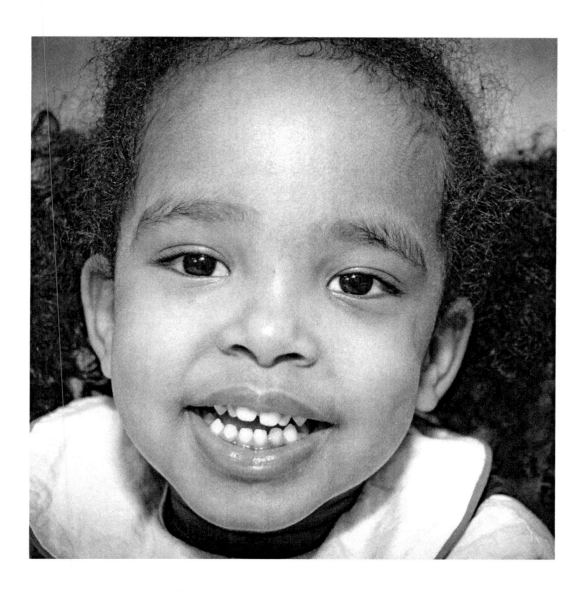

A Matthew House in Your Town?

Recently, as I drove back to Toronto from Windsor, with tears in my eyes, I kept thinking, "Would to God every church had a Matthew House next door or nearby." Grace Baptist Church has been re-vitalized and grown significantly through its welcome and embrace of new refugees. Pastor Stan Mantle and his wife, Heather, Director of Matthew House, work together to give needed leadership and care. Many of the new immigrants and refugees are Karen Baptists—fruit of the work of a pioneer missionary to Burma, the Rev. Adoniram Judson.

The same has happened at First Baptist Church, Fort Erie. The church is revitalized in recent years largely because they have received new people almost weekly into the Matthew House context, and also into the life of church right next door.

You may know of three Matthew Houses (Toronto, Windsor, Fort Erie). There are now five within the CBOQ. The heart, vision and hard work of Anne Woolger have been catalytic to the beginning of these ministries of welcome. The dream has become reality: actual buildings, real homes. That can happen over and over again in any number of places where God's people catch the vision and make it a reality through their own concerted actions.

Serving with us in CBOQ are Cooperative Baptist Fellowship missionaries Marc and Kim Wyatt. They have been instrumental in helping to stimulate, shape and make real the new centres underway in Ottawa (at Centrepoint House, linked with Bethany Baptist Church) and in Montreal (being established through the good work of Christine Walsh and Christopher Lu).

It makes sense that a Matthew House could be established at the end of the Refugee Highway in the major cities noted here. But why couldn't any CBOQ local church, Association or group of churches, link together to start a new house?

Where a Matthew House is not the right answer, why not a Karen group from Burma, most of whom have agricultural backgrounds? They could be welcomed into our rural churches. Several new families would bring vitality and blessing to a small church. Declining churches could come newly alive if they imagined and responded by creating a place of welcome for the stranger and foreigner who are now very near.

Are we ready for the increase of a Haitian diaspora as it arrives "at our doorstep"? Is it enough to send money elsewhere, valid and needed as that is, and not do the pressing and practical things required for those who come to start anew in our country? Many of the Haitian families will come to places close to our homes and churches—and we will have the opportunity to help them start their lives over again.

Too idealistic? Perhaps. But then again, maybe not. Isn't this part of the Gospel of love and care that we proclaim? Can we move beyond speaking the right words to doing the right things?

We are called to join Christ and His People in seeking to "bless all the nations of the earth." I believe that the spreading reality of a Matthew House Movement in CBOQ is part of that. You can help make Matthew Houses more than wonderful theory, more than a wonderful project happening somewhere else.

I invite you, your church, local partnerships and your Association, to get in on the blessing.

Rev. Dr. Laurie Barber, *Director of Missional Initiatives, CBOQ*

ABOUT THE AUTHOR

Joey Clifton is a freelance author and photographer with a passion for missions, ministry and Christian education. He is a graduate of The Southern Baptist Theological Seminary where he earned a Masters in Religious Education and a Ph.D. in Christian Education. Joey has served churches in Kentucky, Alabama, Tennessee and Oklahoma as staff educator. He also has been Adjunct Professor at Memphis Theological Seminary and Indiana University, Southeast. He currently lives with his wife, Jennie, in Norman Oklahoma and is an active member of First Baptist Church, Oklahoma City. In recent years, Joey and Jennie participated in numerous short-term mission trips that have taken them to Africa, Asia and Central America. Before this project, he authored Christian education articles, devotions, Bible study curriculum and books on missions. You can see more of Joey's work at: www.joeyclifton.com.

ENDORSEMENTS

"The Matthew House Story" is a beautiful account of how God works through ordinary people to perform extraordinary ministry. It's a compelling book that tells how communities of individuals, churches and organizations have worked together to create holistic, sustainable ministries to refugees. I was inspired and challenged.

Daniel Vestal
Executive Coordinator
Cooperative Baptist Fellowship
Atlanta, Georgia USA

Reading through the vision of the Matthew House movement, you will be drawn into the story of God's people; women, men and communities and you'll feel compelled to join. Since its beginning, the relationship between Baptist Women and Matthew Houses has been a two-way street of blessing, encouragement and opportunity. Give thanks as you read the names of Anne, Kim, Nancy, Shirley, Joanne, Heather, Jan, Christina and many more. Maybe your name will be in the next telling.

Brenda Mann
Executive Director
Canadian Baptist Women of Ontario and Quebec
Toronto, Ontario, Canada

Anyone interested in the mission of God and the renewal of the North American church should read this book. Matthew House Christians have discovered an imminently practical, culturally relevant way to live out the Biblical injunctions to "welcome the stranger" and serve "the least of these." I pray the Matthew House ministry becomes a Movement that spreads across Canada, throughout the United States and wherever refugees seek safety and need the presence of Christ. Our churches just might need Matthew House even more than refugees do.

Larry Hovis
Executive Coordinator
Cooperative Baptist Fellowship of North Carolina
Winston-Salem, North Carolina

A remarkable story of how the vision of one woman to establish Matthew House changed the lives of thousands of people on the Refugee Highway. In return, their stories of hope and courage, in spite of very difficult circumstances, reveal the goodness of God's love and grace. And the story goes on...."

Nancy Webb
Former Executive Director 1997 - 2005
Canadian Baptist Women of Ontario and Quebec
Toronto, Ontario, Canada

The story of Anne Woolger's vision for Matthew House, and its subsequent birth and development into a Movement, is a touching and compelling one. But that story is quickly enveloped by the myriad of individual stories of refugees that have been warmly welcomed and lovingly cared for, many of them nothing short of miraculous in the way God guided them to the safe and loving environment of a Matthew House. It is also a story of the rewards of giving, as the lives of so many volunteers and staff are deeply impacted and enriched through their friendships with the refugees that they serve. Matthew House is one of the best examples I know of Christians who "show their faith by what they do" (James 2:18)

L. Blair Clark
Associate General Secretary
Canadian Baptist Ministries
Mississauga, Ontario, Canada

Matthew House takes Jesus at his word—when you welcome strangers, you welcome God into your midst. Canada is richer for the excellent settlement assistance that refugee claimants access through Matthew House ministries. Thousands of well-established Canadians have been challenged and blessed through their friendship with newcomers who, overcoming adversity and hardship, work to make Canada their home.

Hugh Brewster
National Manager
Canadian Programs
World Vision Canada

The story of Matthew House is the story of a movement of people and the amazing leadership of a woman of substance and faith - Anne Woolger. You don't stand long in her presence without realizing that her leadership is God breathed and shaped by the servant leadership of Jesus. Read this book and you will realize that while this Matthew House movement continues, it points the way that churches and followers of Jesus can start with a 'mustard seed mentality' and make a difference. We are proud that Anne is an alumni of Tyndale and cut her teeth in refugee ministry as a student at the seminary.

Gary V. Nelson
President and Vice Chancellor
Tyndale University College & Seminary

I recall choking back tears of emotion as Anne Woolger related the story of a refugee family being reunited after arriving several years apart seeking a place at Matthew House. The sister came not even realizing her brothers were still alive, but Anne recognized the family connection and was able to bring them together with little further delay. The Matthew House movement is full of amazing stories like that. So many of us have been inspired by Anne's vision and passion. This book will give you a small glimpse of the daily miracles that continue as dedicated workers carry on this wonderful ministry. Read, and let your heart be warmed and your will prompted to action.

Ken Bellous
President, Canadian Baptist Ministries
Former Executive Minister
Canadian Baptists of Ontario and Quebec

The Matthew House Story is much more than an account of ministry to refugees in Canada. It's a story of ministry in the twenty-first century, an account of what can happen when followers of Jesus Christ have a dream and motivate others to join them in that dream. It's a story of partnership and mutual collaboration.

And it demonstrates that global missions today has as much to do with people who live among us as it has to do with people who live on the other side of the world. This is a story that can create passion within followers of Jesus Christ to minister to the most neglected in their midst. Read it and make it a model for ministry in your context.

This is a great read!

Rob Nash
Professor of Missions and World Religions
McAfee School of Theology
Mercer University
Atlanta, GA

CPSIA information can be obtained at www.ICGtesting.com
Printed in the USA
LVOW070410190512

282368LV00002B/3/P

9 780981 014913